The Propagation of
Alpine Plants and Dwarf Bulbs

Brian Halliwell

The Propagation of Alpine Plants and Dwarf Bulbs

B. T. Batsford Ltd · London

© 1992 Brian Halliwell

Line illustrations by Eilidh Reeves

First published 1992 by B. T. Batsford Ltd,
4 Fitzhardinge Street, London W1H 0AH

ISBN 0–7134–7019–4

A CIP catalogue record for this book is available from the British
Library

Typeset by Paston Press, Loddon, Norfolk
Printed and bound in Great Britain by Billings, Worcester

Contents

Part Two: Recommended Propagation Methods for Individual Plants

Figures

Preface

There are many reasons why any gardener should propagate plants. For most beginners it is a necessity, as lack of money precludes the purchase of many plants. As gardeners become more experienced, they may find that many of the plants they want are not available commercially, and growing from seed or cuttings is the only way to obtain them.

Propagation is also a means of insurance. Single plants can be easily lost through disease or a severe winter; by creating a few extra plants and keeping them in a frame or by giving them to friends, replacements are at hand if disaster strikes.

Another important conservation aspect of propagation is ensuring that stocks in the wild are not depleted. The more plants grown in cultivation, the less likely that plants will be removed from their native habitats.

There are some gardeners to whom propagation is the whole *raison d'être* of gardening; they revel in producing a plant from what appears to be no more than a speck of dust or a small slip of wood. These enthusiasts aside, there can be few gardeners who do not get a thrill from seeing the first green leaves breaking the surface, particularly with the first pot of the season.

There are many alpine and rock garden societies that the enthusiast can join. As well as providing a wealth of information in their magazines and other publications, these societies also hold seed exchanges in which members donate seed collected from their gardens or in the wild to a central organiser, who produces a list from which all members are able to select a number of packets. The last Alpine Garden Society list (1990) ran to 5409 items, which shows the wealth of material open to those wanting to propagate.

Besides this, many commercial firms offer seed for sale and there are always advertisements at the back of alpine journals for seed-collecting expeditions to various parts of the world. The latter source adds an extra dimension to the excitement of propagation by offering the possibility of growing something that no-one has ever attempted before.

There has not been a detailed volume on propagation of alpine plants since the publication of Lawrence D. Hills' famous book *The Propagation of Alpines* in 1950. This has been out of print for some time, with second-hand copies eagerly sought by enthusiasts. But much has happened since 1950. New techniques have been developed, and many new plants have become available to the grower; Hills listed 430 genera, this work offers over 2000.

Whereas Hills directed his volume specifically at growers in the British Isles, this book has been written for gardeners living in any country in a temperate region. For this reason, when giving times of the year, seasons rather than months have been specified. The list of genera includes those that are widely grown in some countries but which may be unknown in others. Mention of cultivation in alpine houses, shade houses or basements using artificial light has been avoided, but information can be found in Robert Rolfe's excellent book, *The Alpine House*.

Acknowledgements

During my professional life I was fortunate in visiting many countries to see alpine plants in the wild. Having worked in both hemispheres I have gained a wide experience of growing and propagating alpines in different climates. It has been possible to inspect facilities at many botanic gardens and other horticultural institutions and to discuss techniques with their staff. Information has been acquired from many alpine enthusiasts, both amateur and professional, in many countries. From discussions I have had with them, I have gained experience in solving propagation problems. The names of all these people are too numerous for me to remember them individually, so I hope that no one will feel slighted if theirs is omitted.

There are some, however, to whom I would like to convey my thanks: Tony Hall, who is responsible for propagation of alpines at the Royal Botanic Gardens Kew. Brian Mathew of the Kew Herbarium, both as a botanist and a horticulturist. Susyn Andrews of the Kew Herbarium, who has helped me with plant names. Ron McBeath, Assistant Curator of the Alpine Department at the Royal Botanic Gardens, Edinburgh. Graham Rice, who has provided advice on the layout of this book. Alan Cook, who until retirement was in charge of the rock garden at Kew and who has grown and propagated many of the plants mentioned in this book. He has checked the text for me, picking up numerous errors and has made many helpful suggestions. Eilidh Reeves who has produced the line drawing from my clumsy scribbles.

Part One

Techniques

1 Seed Propagation

There are two methods of plant propagation: sexual or seed and asexual or vegetative. Although seed is a very popular way of propagating plants it is not the most accurate. A seed results from the fertilisation of the female cell within the ovary by the male from the pollen grain. Seed not only takes the characteristics of the parent from which it is produced, but is also likely to contain elements of its pollen parent and its forebears. It is perhaps useful to list here the various advantages and limitations of propagating from seed, as a broad guideline.

Advantages
—Seed of most species can be stored for long periods without deterioration.
—It is the cheapest way of introducing new plants into a garden.
—In general no special skills or facilities are required.
—Easy to dispatch, it allows exchange with friends or it can be purchased from any specialised seed house.
   Seed can be imported or exported with minimum documentation. This allows a gardener to obtain another country's plants from seed exchanges or from amateur or professional collectors. Plants, on the other hand, are subject to strict and prolonged quarantine control and when moved between the hemispheres considerable skills are required to keep them alive until they have readjusted to the change in seasons. This does not occur with the seedlings produced from imported seed.
—It enables the production of new kinds of plants: selection of seedlings can produce plants with improved performance, greater resistance to disease and weather and with flowers, foliage and fruits of different quality, colour, form or season.
—Hybrids can be produced from the crossing of different species.
—Healthier progeny results because few diseases are transmitted.

Limitations
—Not all plants produce seed because of: time of flowering; adverse weather conditions; stamens and/or stigma that have become petaloid in double flowers; and plants of only one sex being grown when the species is dioecious.
—Variation can be so great that seedlings bear little resemblance to their parent. Some genera (such as *Aquilegia*) are so promiscuous that it is

3

difficult, if not impossible, to keep a species true when a number of different ones are being grown together in a garden.

—It can take a long time for some plants raised from seed to reach flowering due to complex germination requirements and extended periods of juvenility.

—Seedlings of most variegated plants will have green leaves.

For successful germination it is necessary to have viable seed, water, oxygen and a suitable temperature. A common reason for failure to obtain germination is that the seed is in fact dead before it is sown. For a viable seed to be produced, pollination followed by fertilisation must have taken place.

Many plants grown in the rock garden come from mountainous regions where bad weather can be common at flowering time, which prevents pollen from being transferred from anther to stigma. In some species male and female flowers appear on different plants. This is common with many New Zealand plants and occurs in the Northern Hemisphere in such genera as *Ilex*, *Salix* and *Skimmia*. Plants of both sexes need to be present and in close proximity for pollination to take place. It can happen that there are plants of one sex only in some gardens.

Self sterility is a condition that can occur in a plant when pollen will not fertilise its own ovules. Whilst this condition will occur within a single plant, it can also occur in others which have been vegetatively propagated from it, for example *Diascia* species.

Whilst adverse weather conditions can prevent pollination from taking place, even when pollen does land on the stigma, external conditions may totally or partially prevent fertilisation from occurring. It requires only one ovule to be fertilised for a fruit to develop, so that within that fruit there can be a mixture of fertile and infertile seed. This is especially common with species in family Myrtaceae. Although with many plants it is obvious when no seed has been set, in others, for example *Pinus* and *Clematis* species, apparently good seed can develop, but within the testa there is no embryo.

Even when fertilisation has been successful, insects can attack the seed. Adult females insert eggs into the developing seed and the resulting larvae feed on the embryo and stored foods. Such damage is more usual on larger seed and can be common on species within Compositae and Leguminosae. If such damage is suspected, examine the seed with a magnifying glass, looking for a minute hole.

Seed may be collected before it is fully developed, which can occur due to lack of experience. In some plants, such as species within Myrtaceae, Pinaceae and Cupressaceae, it can take a year or more for seed to be fully developed following pollination. When collecting from the wild, seed has to be taken with the hope that it is sufficiently developed for germination to take place.

Fully mature fertile seed may have a short period of viability so that by the time seed is sown it may already be dead. Viability can vary from a few days—as with willows and poplars (cottonwood)—to many decades. When ideal

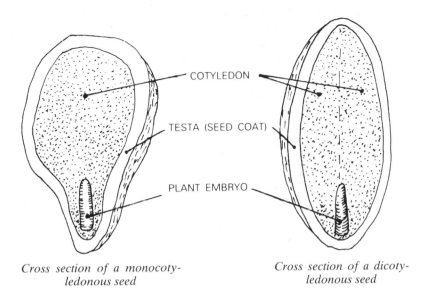

COTYLEDON

TESTA (SEED COAT)

PLANT EMBRYO

Cross section of a monocotyledonous seed

Cross section of a dicotyledonous seed

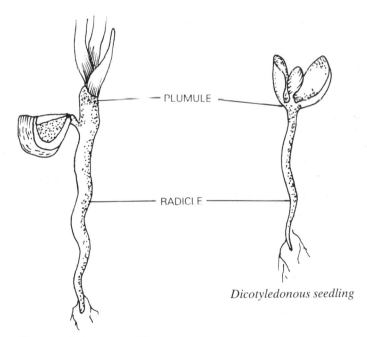

PLUMULE

RADICLE

Dicotyledonous seedling

Monocotyledonous seedling

Figure 1   Monocotyledonous and dicotyledonous seedlings

5

conditions for germination were provided for seeds of a species of *Nelumbo* thought to have laid buried in a Manchurian peat bog for more than a thousand years, germination took place. Adverse storage conditions, such as high temperatures or currents of moving air, can reduce viability. In general seed requires dry storage but some, such as the seed of certain bog plants, perennials or trees, need moist storage. For instance, if seed of *Helleborus* species is stored dry, germination is sparse, long delayed or can fail to take place at all. Seed requiring moist storage should be sown immediately it is collected, but when this is not possible it should be stored cold in moist sphagnum moss or peat. The viability of any seed, but especially that with a short life, can be extended by keeping seed packages in waterproof containers in a refrigerator.

A gardener has no knowledge of the age of seed unless he or she has personally collected it. Much seed from commercial sources is likely to be a year old before it is sold. Some seed obtained from seed exchanges can be a year or more old, especially if the list includes species obtained from the other hemisphere. However, the seed obtained from or through collectors, whether amateur or professional, is unlikely to be more than three months old, as usually every effort is made to clean, packet and distribute it within weeks of collection. All seed should be sown as soon possible after receipt, and if this is not possible stored in the best conditions possible: a drawer in a cool, dry room or in a waterproof packet within a refrigerator.

Water, which is necessary to soften the contents of a dry seed, and oxygen are essential for germination to take place. As germination will not occur if temperatures are too low (i.e. below freezing point), neither will it occur if too high—for example, lettuce seed will not germinate if temperatures rise above 78°F (25°C). For many alpine plants, seed will germinate when temperatures rise a few degrees above freezing. Temperatures to be provided for the majority of plants grown on a rock garden need not exceed 60°F (15°C).

Light can be an important factor in germination. In nature many seeds germinate in the dark after being covered with soil or vegetable debris. It is common practice when sowing seed to cover it with a thin layer of soil. However, germination of seed of most mountain plants seems to be stimulated by light.

Dormancy

In some seed there are regulating mechanisms to ensure that seed germinates when prevailing climatic conditions are favourable to development of the seedling. This regulating factor is known as dormancy and its cause must be overcome before germination will take place. There are three types of dormancy: hard seed coat, an embryo condition and chemical inhibitors.

Seedcoat Dormancy
A hard seed coat develops during the ripening process and is most common in regions with hot and dry summers. Seed with hard seed coats cannot imbibe

water so the contents within remain dry and germination is unable to take place even when there is abundant soil moisture. In nature the testa will gradually break down after attacks by soil fungi and bacteria. This can take varying amounts of time, so germination of a batch of seed takes place over a considerable period, thus reducing competition at any one time.

Another way by which seed coats can be damaged is by acids within the digestive tracts of birds and browsing animals. Following excretion such seed will be able to germinate. Movement of birds and animals helps in the dissemination of the species.

Forest, bush or grass fires are common in some parts of the world. The charring of the testa will allow the seed to take up water when the next rains arrive. As fire will have destroyed the surrounding vegetation the resulting seedlings can develop without competition.

To speed up germination of seed exhibiting seed coat dormancy, the gardener has to damage the testa artificially. Many books suggest that this can be done by filing or chipping the testa, but this can be tedious and uncomfortable and is practical only with large seed. An easier method is to mix seed with dry sharp sand or gravel in a container with a screw-top lid and to shake vigorously. This action results in abrasions to the testa. The treated seed can be separated from sand or gravel by sieving, or alternatively the seed can be sown with the sand.

Acid treatment also recommended in some books is dangerous both to gardener and seed. In no two years are weather conditions the same and so testa thickness and hardness varies and it is virtually impossible to draw up a table for length of treatment; too short a time has little beneficial effect; too long damages or kills the embryo. Much the safest and the easiest way of dealing with seedcoat dormancy is by hot water treatment. Pour boiling water over the seed and allow it to steep for 24 hours in the cooled water before sowing.

Embryo Dormancy

Warm autumn/fall rains could result in fallen seed germinating, with resulting seedlings being killed by severe winter frosts. To guard against this there is a condition within the embryo that prevents germination from taking place until winter has passed and warm spring weather has arrived. If seed with embryo dormancy is kept in a glasshouse where temperatures remain permanently at 60°F (15°C) it will never germinate. In the garden, seed that exhibits embryo dormancy should be sown in containers and then stood out of doors to be exposed to winter cold, with germination expected in the spring. Whilst frost and/or snow are beneficial they are not essential to break embryo dormancy; for most seed 40°F (5°C) is low enough. Germination can be hastened in seed received from the other hemisphere by putting the container in which the seed has been sown into a polythene bag and placing it in a refrigerator for eight weeks before transferring it to gentle warmth. For the dormancy factor to

7

break down the seed must be moist when it is exposed to the cold; it is not enough simply to put the packet of seed into the refrigerator for a few weeks.

Sometimes parts of an embryo need different conditions to develop. In some, for example a number of species of *Lilium* and all *Paeonia*, a period of warmth is needed for the radicle to emerge, but the plumule does not appear until after it has experienced winter cold. After autumn/fall sowing, the container should be kept in a frame or glasshouse and when the radicle emerges the container transferred outside where it should remain over winter. The plumule will then emerge in spring as temperatures rise. Germination of this kind of seed can be hastened by placing the container after sowing in the warmth until the radicle has emerged, and then transferring it for eight weeks to a refrigerator.

There is a group of plants that includes species of *Sanguinaria*, *Smilacina*, *Convallaria*, *Polygonatum* and *Trillium* which has even more complex germination requirements. Seed of these species needs a period of warmth followed by cold for the radicle to appear, with a second period of warmth followed by cold before the plumule emerges. Following late summer or autumn/fall sowing, the germination of seeds of these plants will not be complete in less than two years. It does not seem possible to hasten the germination of any seed within this group of moving containers between glasshouse and refrigerator. Probably if any spell is too short, the whole process is negated.

Chemical Inhibitors

There can be chemicals present in the external covering or within the seed which will prevent germination from taking place. Such inhibitors prevent the seed from germinating whilst still within its fruits. In nature pulp is removed in the digestive tract of animals or birds after being eaten, or if it falls to the ground it will decompose as it is attacked by bacteria or fungi. Before sowing seed that has a fleshy fruit, it should be extracted by maceration and washed clean; if not sown immediately it can be dried and stored.

Inhibitors can be present within the seed of many desert plants. In desert regions there are often heavy dews daily and occasional showers. If germination were to occur in such periods the resulting seedlings would shrivel and die when the meagre amount of water had evaporated. Prolonged rain will wash out the inhibitor so that germination can occur and seedlings are assured of sufficient soil moisture to establish before drought returns. Under cultivation seed that is known to contain inhibitors should be soaked for 24 hours in cold water before being sown. In many kinds of seed containing inhibitors, the active chemical ingredient breaks down naturally. In seeds of many species of *Primula*, for example, germination takes a long time if seed is sown immediately after collection; but if delayed for four weeks germination is immediate.

It can also happen that seed exhibits more than one kind of dormancy: in species of *Ceanothus* there can be a hard seed coat and embryo dormancy. In *Rosa* there can be a chemical inhibitor in the fruit and both a hard seed coat and embryo dormancy. Seed of some plants that contain chemical inhibitors or have hard seed coats will germinate almost immediately if sown when fully developed but before the ripening process is complete. Many buttercups, species of *Ranunculus*, if collected when the seed is dark brown will take up to two years to germinate, whereas if the seed is sown when still green it can germinate within a few weeks. Cyclamen seed sown immediately the pods have burst will germinate within three or four weeks but if stored for a long time before sowing can take many months. This speed-up of germination occurs because the seed is sown before the chemical inhibitor has been laid down. Many legumes if sown whilst the seed is soft will germinate almost immediately, as they will after a wet summer.

Unfortunately, dormancy cannot be predicted. Reference books may help with plants that have been long in cultivation but for recently introduced plants nothing is likely to be recorded. Legumes must be expected to have seed coat dormancy. Mountain plants from the Northern Hemisphere are likely to have embryo dormancy. This condition, however, is confined to certain families and must be expected in all members of Rosaceae. Whereas embryo dormancy is to be expected in mountain plants of the Northern Hemisphere it does not seem to occur in Southern Hemisphere alpines, although cold does stimulate germination so that more seedlings appear quickly and together rather than erratically over a long period. If dormancy occurs in one species of a genus it must be expected in others, although this does not always occur: for example, only some species of *Lilium* have delayed germination.

Seeds can be temperamental. In some where one expects dormancy, germination can be immediate, and yet in others where no dormancy is usual seed can be long delayed in germinating. The germination responses in some seed can be quite different from the norm in certain years. There are many apparent germination failures because containers are discarded too early. No seed container should be discarded in less than a year, even those where immediate germination is expected. Two years is even better, and for those where dormancy is known to exist three or even four years. There are records of seed of some species of New Zealand *Ranunculus*, where normally germination cannot be expected in under two years, still germinating a few at a time over a period of ten years.

When nothing is known about the seed and no records are to be found in any publication, sow the seed on receipt, plunge immediately out of doors and wait patiently.

Sowing Seed

Amounts of seed of alpines to be sown will never be large. Thus, containers in which this seed is to be sown can be 3, 4 or 5in (75, 100 or 125mm) in diameter. It is preferable to choose one size for convenience and to use two or more smaller pots for larger amounts of seed.

For seed that is going to take six months or more to germinate, clay or plastic pots are preferable, but old food or drink containers made of plastic, waxed paper or polystyrene can be used for seed that germinates within a few weeks. Whatever container is used it must be clean, with enough drainage holes to take away surplus water. Often it is recommended to put into the pot drainage material in the form of broken crocks or coarse gravel, but this is necessary only if there are inadequate drainage holes or the garden is in an area of high rainfall.

It will be more convenient for gardeners to purchase their seed-sowing composts ready mixed from garden centres. There are many kinds available of varying qualities and it may be necessary to shop around. Those based solely on peat can be used for quick-germinating seed but are not to be recommended for seed where germination is long delayed or where containers are to be plunged out of doors. Peat or pulverised bark that is mixed with sand can be used, but a soil-based compost is to be preferred. The best composts are those made up to the John Innes seed formula in which the soil has been sterilised. For gardeners who cannot obtain a reliable ready mixed compost or prefer to prepare their own, the following is reliable:

2 parts soil
1 part peat or leaf mould
1 part sharp sand
(all parts by volume).

The soil to be used is best sterilised to kill weed seeds, soil pests and disease organisms. This process can be carried out in a kitchen. Take a large saucepan with a tight fitting lid, add $\frac{1}{2}$in (12mm) of water and bring to the boil. Meanwhile pass a quantity of dry soil through a $\frac{1}{2}$in (10mm) sieve to remove lumps and stones and add to the boiling water. Replace the lid and simmer on the lowest heat for 15 minutes. Remove the pan from the heat, empty the soil onto a clean surface and spread it out so it can cool quickly. Peat should be sterile, but if leaf mould is to be used, which contains many weed seeds, this too should be sterilised. Use a coarse sand with particle size up to $\frac{1}{8}$in (2.5mm); avoid builder's sand, sea sand, sand with clay or shell grit. Mix the ingredients together thoroughly and store in clean polythene bags until required. Sterilise ingredients separately and only enough for immediate use.

Fill the chosen container to the top and firm with the fingers so that the final surface is $\frac{1}{2}$in (12mm) below rim level. Level off the surface using a flattener (see figure); failing this, use the flat base of another pot. Onto this surface sow the seed evenly and thinly, either directly from the packet or by taking a pinch and letting it dribble over the surface. More even sowing can be achieved with very fine seed by mixing it with a quantity of dry fine soil or sand. If flowers of sulphur are used instead, it is easier to see the rate of sowing and this chemical also provides some protection against disease organisms. Over-thick sowing is very common and results in crowded seedlings that become drawn and liable to suffer from damping-off diseases. Sow two or even three pots rather than try to crowd too much seed into one container. As there is better germination of

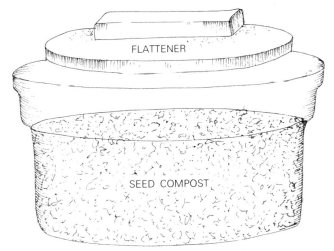

Pot filled with seed compost

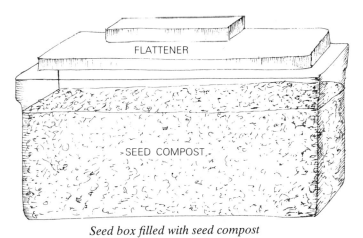

Seed box filled with seed compost

Figure 2   *Pot and seed box filled with seed compost*

alpine seed if exposed to light the seed should not be covered with more seed compost. Instead use a coarse sand from which the dust has been sieved out; take a quantity in the hand and scatter it over the surface of the seed compost thin enough to be able to see the seed between the grains. The sand will reduce surface drying, prevent fine seed from being splashed out of the pot and discourage moss and liverworts. With seed having immediate germination, a fine covering of seed compost can be used. Large seed can be spaced out or sown singly in pots, pressed into the compost and covered.

Having sown the seed put a label in the pot. Never rely on your memory—it's never as good as you think! If you are sowing lots of pots which may take up to two years to germinate there is no possibility that you will be able to remember what has been sown. Labels can be made of a number of kinds of material. The best is the metal type on which an ordinary lead pencil can be used. There are many types of plastics of varying thicknesses, durability and surfaces. On some an ordinary pencil can be used, but with others it has to be some kind of ink. Use a waterproof ink that does not fade with exposure to the sun—those with an alcohol base are suitable. There are wooden labels sold in shops, and substitutes such as spatulas or ice-cream or lolly sticks. All these should be covered with matt white paint to extend their life, making a smoother surface on which to write and extending the time that the writing remains legible. The basic information to put onto a label is genus, species and, where applicable, sub-species, variety or cultivar. If there is a collector's number with the seed this must go onto the label even if there is both genus and species. Many gardeners keep records in notebooks of seed sown, where additional information can be recorded: for example, date of sowing, compost and source; and subsequently date of germination, dormancy details and percentage of germination. Such information is valuable for future sowings or to pass to friends. Once the seed has been sown ensure the container is watered by rosed can and continue to apply water at regular intervals.

Seed that is known to germinate immediately should not be sown until spring when temperatures are rising. If heat is available, sowing can be brought forward to late winter, but it must be ensured that once the seedlings appear daylight is improving. High temperatures are unnecessary and 60°F (15°C) is quite adequate; if seed is being germinated in unheated glasshouses, tunnels, frames or on the kitchen window-sill germination will take longer. There is no disadvantage if temperatures fluctuate, as they do between day and night; in fact this is an advantage. To reduce drying out, sheets of glass or polythene should be put over the seed containers, which may be shaded with sheets of newspapers in sunny weather. The glass or polythene should be turned daily so that condensation does not drip onto the seeds. Uncover any containers as soon as germination takes place. If seed has not germinated after six weeks transfer the container outside and plunge.

When there is known delayed germination or with new or unknown seed, containers should be put outside where they will be exposed to winter cold. Such containers should be plunged to their rim in ashes, sand, peat or pulverised bark. Plunging keeps pots from falling over, reduces drying out, and prevents clay pots from cracking or flaking in frosty weather and plastic pots from cracking or splitting. A plunge area can be in any open part of the garden or in frames where there is no impeded drainage. Dig out the soil to a depth of 6–8 in (150–200m), add at least 2in (50mm) of broken stone, brick or coarse gravel for drainage and then cover with a layer of sharp sand to provide a firm even base. The pots are then placed on top. Square plastic pots will fit tightly together, but round pots should be packed with plunge material in the spaces between.

Following plunging, protection will be needed against birds, which scratch in pots and pull out labels, or mice, which burrow down to eat the seed. In areas of high rainfall some protection in the form of lights, clear plastic or stretched polythene will be needed. Even with a covering of sand or gravel on the seed compost, moss can still appear. Unless this forms a solid mat through which rain penetrates with difficulty, it is better left.

Liverworts are a real nuisance, being especially troublesome where rainfall is high. These can completely cover pots, restricting water penetration and preventing seedlings from emerging. Ideally these ought to be picked out of the pots, but where there are large numbers this is tedious and inconvenient. Spraying with a fungicide such as Benlate will kill the liverworts but may leave a slimy mess. Weeds can appear in the pots but unless these can be clearly identified it is better to let them stay. Once germination of the sown seed occurs, weeds can be removed before the container is transferred. Don't have pots of ungerminated and germinated seed mixed together in a plunge bed— keep them separated.

Seed of Ericaceae, Gesneriaceae and most species of *Primula* and *Meconopsis* are sensitive to drying out during germination. If the water content of a compost falls below a critical level once the germination process has begun, few seedlings will appear, and in extreme cases none. During seed sowing a modification to the usual process should be made in which the surface of the seed compost is covered with a layer of sphagnum moss. Sphagnum moss, which is sterile, holds 15 times its own weight of water and ensures there will be no drying out. Take a small quantity of dry sphagnum moss and rub it through an ⅛in (2.5mm) sieve, pour boiling water over the sieved moss to kill weed seed and when cool squeeze out any surplus water. Having prepared a seed container with a lime-free compost spread a thin layer of the moss over the surface and sow the seed thinly on this; do not cover.

A modification of this method can be used by people who germinate seed on their kitchen window-sills. Take a clean translucent plastic box—for example, the type used for sandwiches, ice cream or food storage. Place in the bottom a 1in (25mm) layer of moist, lime-free seed compost. Firm, level and cover with a layer of the sieved moss. Sow the seed on top of this, label and replace the tight-fitting lid. At no time should the compost be watered otherwise waterlogging will occur. Light can pass through the plastic, which is waterproof, and condensation on the sides will run back into the compost. Place the box where there is plenty of light but out of direct sun. Do not keep opening the box otherwise the moisture will be lost and drying out can occur. Seedlings, which may be handled when big enough, can stay in the box for up to two years. These containers can be used for raising many kinds of seed with or without moss. If, however, any of the seed has embryo dormancy, put it into a refrigerator for eight weeks before transferring to the window-sill.

Care of Seeds and Seedlings

When raising plants from seed, germination is only part of the process; resulting seedlings have then to become established. Following germination,

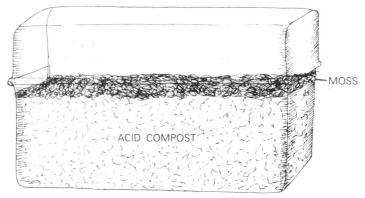

Figure 3   Translucent food container prepared for sowing Rhododendron *seed*

seedlings should be exposed to full light, although it is preferable to keep them out of direct sunlight especially in the early days. At no time should containers lack water. Protect seedlings from depredations by slugs, snails, cockroaches and woodlice. Damping-off diseases are fungal agents which attack seedlings at ground level. Infection is water-borne and usually occurs when watering from barrels, butts or tanks; use direct mains water wherever possible. This condition is always more serious where seedlings are too thick or which have become drawn. If this disease does appear, water with a solution of Captan or Benlate.

When sowing seed, one compost can be used for all; when seedlings are to be grown on, different compost(s) will be needed. There are many commercial formulations of potting composts available from garden centres. These are of varying compositions and qualities. When soil-based, those in which the loam has been sterilised are better. That prepared to the John Innes formula is best and for seedlings choose Potting Compost No. 1. Those based solely on peat should be reserved for strong or quick growers. Whatever compost is chosen do ascertain whether or not it contains lime. For those gardeners who have no access to a garden centre, are unable to find a reliable potting compost or prefer to mix their own the following mixture is suitable.

3 parts of soil (sieved and sterilised)
2 parts of peat or sterilised leaf mould
1 part of sharp sand or fine grit
(all parts by volume).

Modifications of this formula can be made by increasing the sand/gravel or the peat/leaf mould content. For most plants a lime-free soil is best. Even lime lovers will thrive as long as the pH is not too low. If, however, plants are known to grow better in an alkaline soil (for example, encrusted saxifrages) some lime, in the form of hydrated lime or ground chalk can be added to the compost. It may be preferred to replace the sand/gravel either totally or partially with limestone chippings. There is need for a growing-on compost to have an adequate supply of mineral nutrients. Even when large quantities of compost are mixed, the amounts of hoof and horn (or nitrogen source) superphosphate or sulphate of potash are measured in ounces/grams per bushel/cubic metre. As quantities used by an alpine gardener are very much smaller, rarely more than a bucketful, the amounts of fertilisers become so small that they cannot be weighed out on conventional scales. A dusting of the compost with bonemeal will be adequate for most plants. A safe and easy way of enriching a potting compost is to crush a suitable number of house-plant feeding tablets.

For Ericaceae and plants from mountain moorland or woodland floor, a more organic soil will be required:

    1 part lime-free sterilised soil
    1 part peat
    1 part sharp sand
    (all parts by volume).

Little additional nutrients will be needed, although a dusting of bonemeal is desirable.

Containerisation

Pots with drainage holes are the receptacles most used for growing on seedlings; they can be of either unglazed clay or plastic. Plastic pots are available in different colours, and are either square or round; they are of varying qualities and cost. The cheapest are not always a wise buy, for they can become brittle quite quickly and prolonged exposure to sunlight causes them to crack or break when handled. There are pots made of peat, which expand when soaked and which can be used for quick-maturing plants. After transferring seedlings to these kind of containers, pack them into flats/trays to aid handling. As soon as the roots emerge from their sides, plants should be potted on or planted out. Paper, composition and waxed cardboard containers are also manufactured for growing seedlings. Alternatives are drinks containers of styrafoam or plastic, and food containers can also be used if clean and provided with drainage holes. The diameter of containers for growing on seedlings will vary between 2½ and 3½in (60–90mm), using the smaller for slow growers and the larger for the fast or strong growers.

Handling

The time for handling seedlings will depend on the protection available. In a glasshouse or tunnel, where it is possible to control temperatures, pricking off should be as soon as seedlings are big enough to handle. Even when there is no temperature control, strong growers or those that develop quickly are also better pricked off as soon as the seedlings are big enough to handle. Ensure that the compost within the seed container is moist; if not, water some hours before

15

potting is to take place so that the seedlings will be dry. Invert the container, tap sharply so that the contents slide out; if tins have been used they may have to be cut away. Shake the soil ball gently so that the compost falls away from the seedlings and each can be easily separated. Except in areas of high rainfall, no drainage material, in the form of gravel or broken crocks, need be put into the container.

Some growers put a piece of plastic or zinc gauze in the bottom of the pot to keep out worms. Overfill the container with compost, tap several times to settle and remove any excess. With the pointed end of a narrow dibber or pencil make a hole in the centre of the compost. This should be deep enough for the tip of the radicle to touch the bottom of the hole and the cotyledons to rest on the surface. Holding the seedling between the thumb and forefinger push the soil back into the hole and tap the pot so that the compost settles and leaves a level surface; subsequent watering will ensure that the roots/radicle and soil are in contact. Remember that no root can grow through a hole in the soil, so it is important that radicle and roots along their full length are in touch with soil particles.

When there is no control over heat it will be easier to handle seedlings later when they are bigger; this can be late summer when growth for the year has finished or early the following spring just before growth recommences. When the soil ball is removed from its container, it is probable that there will be sizeable root systems to the seedlings which should be carefully disentangled. If possible the seedling can be inserted into its pot using a dibber as already described, but the root system is likely to be too extensive for this to be practical. Add some compost to the bottom of a container. Holding the seedling between thumb and forefinger, position it in the centre of the pot. With the other hand add more compost around the roots, tapping as the pot fills so that roots and soil are in contact with each other. When filled, firm the compost with the fingers so that the soil surface is $\frac{1}{2}$in (12mm) from the rim; subsequent watering will settle the soil.

Ensure that each kind of seedlings has at least one label per batch; it is preferable, even desirable, to have a label in each pot. A plant without a label and which is unknown is of little value. The initial and early waterings of potted seedlings should be through a rose attached to watering can or hosepipe. When the soil has settled and roots have filled their pots, it will be possible to remove the rose but it is important to control the water pressure.

As soon as seedlings have established in their containers, they should be transferred from glasshouse or tunnel outside to frames or plunge areas. In some areas protection may be needed against excessive rain; this can be in the form of lights when pots are in frames. For plunge beds, sheets of transparent plastic or taut polythene can be securely fixed above the pots ensuring there is no sag. There should be enough space above the pots to allow for air circulation and to prevent temperature build-up. In areas with hot summers it may be necessary to provide protection from the sun, essential with Ericaceae, species of *Primula* and most woodland and moorland plants. Protection can be in the form of plastic shading mesh stretched over a frame or pots can be grown on benches or in plunge areas within bush or shade houses.

Protection must also be provided against pests and diseases. Pests will include aphids, red spiders, caterpillars, leaf-eating beetles, and weevils, capsid or leaf miners, all of which affect aerial parts of plants, whilst the roots can be infested by vine weevil, cut worms, millipedes and root aphids. Diseases are most likely to be mildews and root rots.

Depending on rate of growth, seedlings will remain in their containers for one or two years. Care should be taken not to allow plants to become root bound, and to plant out or pot-on before this stage is reached.

2 Vegetative Propagation

In addition to plant increase by seed there is vegetative propagation, where a new plant is produced by using other parts of a plant: stem, leaf or root; both methods will be used by the gardener. The benefits and limitations of this method of propagation are listed below.

Benefits
—Some plants may not produce seed for the following reasons: (a) plants may flower so late in the season that winter cold prevents seed development, for example, *Zauschneria californica (Epilobium canum)*. (b) No seed will be produced if there is a single plant of a dioecious species in a garden, as in, for example, *Aciphylla, Coprosma* and *Cyathodes*. (c) Some plants are self sterile, i.e. they will not produce seed with their own pollen. (d) Most plants with double flowers are unable to produce seed. (e) A plant may have been bred not to flower, for example *Chamaemelium nobile (Anthemis nobilis)* 'Treneague' the non-flowering chamomile used for making lawns.
—As propagules are identical with each other and their parent, there is uniformity.
—Speeding up of flowering.
—Maintenance of cultivars, bud sports, variegation, and improved and resistant forms.

Limitations
—Some plants are difficult to increase by vegetative propagation and a few might be impossible
—More problems occur when transporting vegetative material with increased possibilities of deterioration when there are delays.
—Quarantine regulations restrict or control movement of plants between countries.
—More sophisticated facilities are required and greater skills needed with some kinds of vegetative propagation.
—There is an increased chance of disease transmission.

It is possible that disease transmission is the most serious problem to occur with vegetative propagation. As a virus disease is systemic, all propagules from infected stock will be infected.

The commonest symptoms of a virus are leaf mottling, distortion and loss of vigour; others are failure to bloom, flower distortion or colour breaking; virus-infected plants can be difficult to propagate vegetatively. There are tolerant plants which show no symptoms, but in a garden these provide a source of infection to others which are sensitive. Transmission of virus is mainly by aphids so strict pest control is necessary at all times. Virus-infected plants must be destroyed by burning, no matter how rare. Ensure that all plants introduced into a garden are virus-free.

Bacterial diseases that infect plants are not numerous but one of the more serious is *Erwinia amylovora*, or fireblight, which is confined to woody members of Rosaceae. Leaves on infected branches are blackened as though a blow torch has been aimed at them. At first only a shoot tip or a single branch might be infected but in subsequent years it will spread over the plant and to others. On a rock garden it is the genus *Cotoneaster* that is most likely to be affected. When collecting propagating material try not to take from infected plants. Infection can have spread beyond the area where symptoms are showing, so if you must propagate, select material where there is no brown staining of the wood under the bark.

Most fungal diseases, such as mildew, are easy to spot and again the use of infected material for propagation should be avoided. *Stereum purpureum*, or silver leaf, takes its name from the appearance of foliage of infected species of *Prunus*. In the rock garden only three species of this genus are likely to be grown: *P. pumila*, *P. prostrata* and *P. tenella*. This disease infects other genera in Rosaceae as well as in other families where symptoms may not be as obvious as in *Prunus*. It should be remembered that the disease can have spread beyond the area showing symptoms, so if propagation has to be from an infected plant, or one suspected of being infected, inspect the wood and reject any where wood is stained brown. The only pests unlikely to be recognised are microscopic eelworms of which *Ditelynchus dipsaci*, stem and bulb eelworm, is probably the most important. It attacks a wide range of plants of which, for the rock gardener, the following are the most important: *Phlox*, *Lysimachia*, *Anemone* (mostly the non-tuberous kinds), *Digitalis*, *Narcissus*, *Galanthus*, *Leucojum*, *Chionodoxa* and *Hyacinthus*. The leaves of infested *Phlox* are black or brown and remain attached to the stems, internodes are shortened and there is loss of vigour. This pest attacks only the stems, so healthy plants can be produced by using root cuttings. Symptoms in bulbs are easy to miss for they are not obvious above ground, producing distortion—slight on leaves but marked in flowers. If infested bulbs are cut across there will be brown scales amongst the normal healthy ones. Hot water treatment can control this problem, but the treatment requires such stringent conditions that it is not really suitable for the amateur. The only effective treatment is to destroy infected plants by burning and to make sure that they are not used for propagation.

In nature there are plants that are able to increase naturally by vegetative

19

means as well as by seed. Gardeners can take advantage of this habit by lifting these plants periodically and detaching new plants or rooted portions.

Creeping Stems

Plants that have a prostrate habit produce long stems, and if they come in contact with the ground they will produce adventitious roots at the nodes, for example *Lysimachia nummularia*. In some plants this will occur naturally, whilst in others some help may be needed by pegging down or placing stones on the stems, for example *Vinca minor*.

Figure 4   Prostrate plant

Runners

A specialised form of creeping stem is the runner, where there are long internodes with a plantlet produced terminally. When a new plant was developed it may produce one or more stems with additional plantlets. The best-known example is the strawberry, but amongst the alpines runners can be found on *Androsace sarmentosa* (*see* Fig. 5).

Suckers

Whilst this term applies to unwanted shoots that develop from the rootstock of a grafted plant, it is also applied to a method of vegetative increase. From a mother plant will develop a short stem at or just below ground level with a daughter plant at its end, for example *Ajuga reptans* (*see* Fig. 6).

20

Figure 5   Strawberry, showing runners

Figure 6   Ajuga reptans *with suckers*

Offsets

These are a modified form of sucker and usually occur in plants with a rosette habit. From the base of a mother plant new rosettes develop around the circumference, for examples in *Sempervivum*, *Echeveria* and *Saxifraga panicu-lata*. Many plants that increase by offsets are monocarpic (*see* Fig. 7).

Bulbs

Botanical bulbs are swollen buds where a growing point is surrounded by fleshy scales produced from modified leaf bases, for example *Fritillaria and Narcissus* (*see* Fig. 8).

21

Figure 7   Sempervivum

Corms

A corm is a swollen stem base that is surrounded by a membranous tunic. Beneath the tunic is a well-developed terminal bud with other buds situated below on compressed nodes, for example *Crocus* and *Gladiolus*.

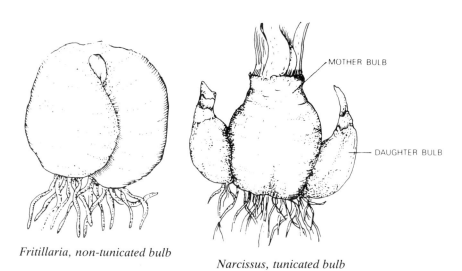

Fritillaria, non-tunicated bulb

Narcissus, tunicated bulb

Figure 8   Fritillaria *and* Narcissus *bulbs*

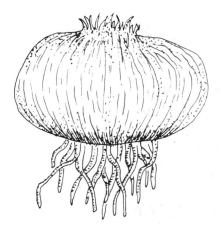

Figure 9 Crocus *corm*

Tubers

A few of these are swollen stems of which the best known is the potato. For the alpine gardener stem tubers are found in a few kinds of *Tropaeolum*, for example *T. polyphyllum*. More important tubers are modified roots. In some

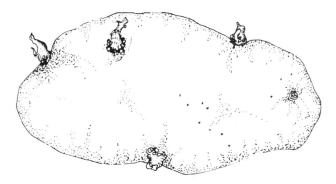

Figure 10   Stem tuber of potato, showing eyes (buds)

the roots are swollen partially, such as *Asphodelus acaulis*, or totally as in *Ranunculus asiaticus*. In others a tap root has become compressed into a rounded or flattened structure with axillary buds on the upper surface, for example in *Anemone blanda* or *Corydalis popovei* (*see* Figs 11 & 12).

Tubercles

Often in plants with a tuberous rootstock miniature swollen structures develop in the leaf axils, for example in *Begonia evansiana*. Alternative names applied to these include tuberlets, bulbets or bulbils.

23

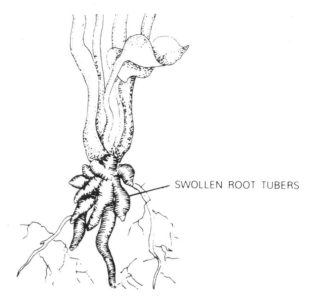

SWOLLEN ROOT TUBERS

Figure 11   Ranunculus asiaticus

Figure 12   *Tuber of* Anemone blanda

Rhizomes

These are modified horizontal stems growing underground or on the surface, from which terminal vertical leafy shoots develop, for example *Iris chamaeiris* or *Convallaria majalis*.

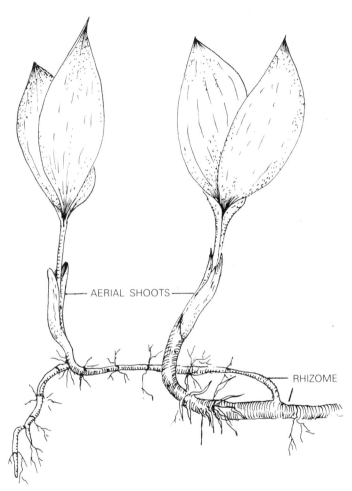

Figure 13   Rhizome of Convallaria majalis

Pseudobulbs

These are modification to stems of orchids that have become swollen with stored food. Amongst the terrestrials most favoured by rock gardeners are species of *Pleione*.

25

Figure 14
Pleione *with pseudobulbs*

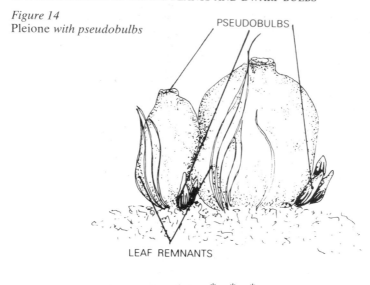

PSEUDOBULBS

LEAF REMNANTS

* * *

The various modified plant organs which are a means of natural vegetative increase are not clearly defined or identifiable. Any of the names can be interchanged for those adaptations for which I have used offset, suckers and runners, and thin rhizomes may be referred to as stolons. In some plants there can be more than one organ which has been modified. In the Juno group of irises, there are root tubers attached to a bulb.

All these methods of vegetative increase will produce new plants naturally, but with man's manipulation this can be greatly increased (*see* Chapter 3).

Division

The easiest method of propagation is by division, which requires no special skills or facilities. It can be carried out on plants with a tufted or suckering habit where there are many shoots rising from a fibrous root system or where there are roots on individual stem bases. It is most usually practised on perennials, for example *Mimulus primuloides*, *Bellis perennis* 'Dresden China' or *Campanula cochlearifolia*, although it can be used for woody plants with a similar habit such as *Chamaebatiaria millefolium*, *Buxus sempervirens* 'Suffruticosa' or *Rosa pimpinellifolia*.

Plants are lifted when not in active growth and divided into two or four pieces or else completely pulled apart into 20 or more individual shoots, each with some roots. A few clumps may be too solid to pull apart and so division will have to be made with a knife, as with *Epimedium* species and cultivars of *Solidago virgaurea*. Division is better carried out every three or four years. It is less productive when dealing with over-large clumps which have not been disturbed for many years, most especially with shrubby subjects. When dividing clumps of any age, discard the oldest central portion where it can be seen there is no new growth or what there is is very weak.

Division may not be possible with plants having a tap root unless there are several crowns and the tap root is short or branched in its upper part. It might be possible to cut through the clump vertically ensuring that the knife passes through the tap root and there is a terminal bud and some fibrous roots. When the tap root is forked in its upper part, each branch can be cut from the main part of the tap root with a terminal bud. These pieces should be lined out in deep pots, boxes/flats or in the open ground with the bud just covered. Eventually the section of root will produce fibrous roots and the terminal bud will start into growth so that at the end of the growing season there is a new plant.

Propagation by Cuttings

The most common method of vegetative propagation is by cuttings. This technique is used by most gardeners at some time to increase plants, with varying degrees of success. With a large number of plants, success can be achieved at most times of the year, although there will be one period when the percentage of rooting is higher. For other plants, cuttings will root only at specific periods which may be limited to one or a few weeks. Timing can therefore be critical! Rather than, say, 4.30 p.m. on 3 July, it is the stage and condition of growth that determines the time for taking cuttings. In a year when there has been a mild winter and growth begins early, the ideal stage of growth can be up to a month earlier than after a later spring.

The amount of sunshine, heat and rainfall at every season can affect rooting, both in the current and the following year. Sunlight builds up the carbohydrates in the plant, which results in a high carbon content. When this is high in relation to the nitrogen level within the plant, rooting will be easier. If, however, there has been a high application of a nitrogenous fertiliser, perhaps to stimulate growth, this can depress rooting. A starved stock plant may provide fewer shoots to make cuttings but what shoots there are will root readily. Cuttings taken in a cool, dull, wet summer will root less successfully than when sunshine figures and temperatures are high. Success will be also poorer when cuttings are taken from a plant grown in deep shade rather than from one in the open. There is even a difference in rooting when cuttings are taken from the inside of a leafy plant instead of from the outside. Strong-growing main stems do not root as successfully as the less vigorous side shoots. Always avoid selecting leaders for propagation. An exception is with some of the conifers with a tiered habit, for example *Abies, Cedrus, Picea* and *Pinus*. If side shoots of these kinds of conifers are rooted, the resulting plants will have a lop-sided habit resulting in asymmetrical trees.

From seed to death, a plant passes through a number of stages of growth: germination, juvenility, adulthood and senescence. Juvenility is the period between germination and flowering. This stage can vary from a few days, as

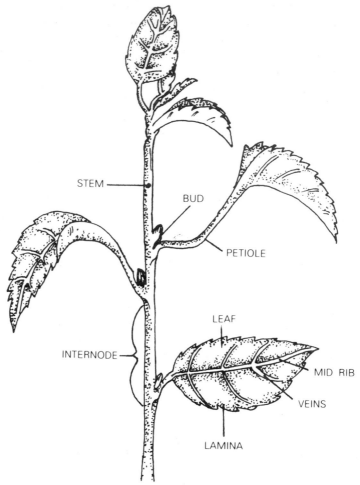

STEM

BUD

PETIOLE

LEAF

INTERNODE

MID RIB

VEINS

LAMINA

Figure 15   Parts of a dicot stem

with annual weeds, to many years: for instance, *Magnolia campbellii* when raised from seed can take 15 years to flower. In most plants there is no marked difference in vegetative growth between the two stages, but with some there are noticeable differences and in a few the two are so unlike that to the inexperienced it may seem that there are two entirely different plants. Whilst this condition is most common in Australasian plants, for example Australian *Eucalyptus perrineana* or New Zealand's *Aciphylla colensoi*, it does occur in the Northern Hemisphere. *Hedera helix* (common or English ivy), in the juvenile state has long unbranched stems with climbing roots and leaves that are deeply lobed. When adult, stems become much branched, there are no stem roots, leaves are almost round and flowering takes place. There are different appearances with many kinds of conifers: juveniles have soft, linear leaves produced around the stem, whilst the adult has hard, scale-like leaves in two dimensions. In many dwarf conifers there have been selections made in which cultivars are either juvenile or adult and there are those that pass from one stage to the other in the usual way.

Cuttings taken from juvenile growth will root better than those taken from the adult. Many plants that are adult can be converted to juvenility by cutting hard. In woody plants this is done by pruning, which should be much harder than usual in a year prior to propagation. It is common practice with perennial rock garden plants or with potted specimens to trim spring bloomers after flowering or with summer or autumn/fall bloomers at the beginning of the growing season. This not only results in a tidier plant, but also produces juvenile growth which will provide excellent cuttings. If an application of fertiliser is given following this cutting back, avoid excessive nitrogen or at least include some potash as a balance.

As plants age, even normally easy plants become increasingly difficult to root, so wherever possible the youngest stock plant should be selected. If propagation of woody plants and reliable perennials is delayed until the plant looks to be in poor condition and is beginning to die of old age, it can be almost impossible to obtain cuttings that will root.

Flowering can also depress the ability of cuttings to root. When selecting propagation material avoid using flowering growth. This can be difficult with plants that have a long flowering season, such as dwarf cultivars or *Fuchsia*, but if a few shoots are cut back hard, new non-flowering growth will be produced. If there are flowers or buds on propagating material these should always be removed during the preparation of the cuttings.

Hardwood Cuttings

This term is used for cuttings of woody plants. Hardwood cuttings are those made from current season's growth in late autumn/fall or winter when growth is complete and wood is mature. There are two sorts of hardwood cuttings: deciduous and evergreen. Only a few rock garden shrubs are deciduous, for example *Salix* species and their cultivars. Cuttings are prepared when shoots have shed their leaves. Take off the current season's growth with a knife or secateurs and cut it into pieces 2–4in (50–100mm) long. Discard the growing point and make the upper cut immediately above a bud and the lower cut immediately below. These can be rooted in the open ground in areas where winters are not severe. Take out a slit with the blade of a spade 1–3in (25mm–75mm) deep and if the soil is heavy add some coarse sharp sand. Push the cuttings in so that their tips just protrude then, using the heel, push the soil firmly against the cuttings. Rooting will have taken place by the following spring when buds will come into growth. Lift at the end of the following autumn/fall when the leaves have fallen and either pot or plant into a permanent position or in a nursery.

When it is impractical to root cuttings in the open ground, they can be inserted around the edge of a pot in a very sandy potting compost where there is good drainage. Keep the pots plunged in an unheated frame. When leaves have fallen from subsequent growth they can be removed from the pot, separated and potted singly.

Cuttings of evergreens can be taken at any time after the cessation of growth in autumn/fall until the winter ends. However, taken too late, bud growth may begin before rooting has taken place when the cuttings usually die.

In mild areas cuttings can be rooted in the open ground, though it is more usual to insert them into pots of rooting medium or line them out in a bed under a frame or in a polythene tunnel. Frames heated from below are preferable for rooting cuttings of *Ilex crenata* and all dwarf conifers. Quick-rooting cuttings, especially when taken early and under protection, can be rooted by late winter when they can be potted. Late-inserted cuttings and slow rooters respond best to having a full growing season before they are lifted for potting.

LOWER LEAVES
REMOVED

Deciduous hardwood cutting

Evergreen hardwood cutting

Figure 16   Evergreen and deciduous hardwood cuttings

Semi-ripe Cuttings

These are taken from shoots that are still in active growth but where the base of the current season's growth is beginning to ripen. Semi-ripe cuttings are taken from mid-summer to early autumn/fall, and protection is needed for their rooting. After preparation, cuttings can be inserted around the edge of pots, put into boxes or lined out in beds of rooting medium. The length of time taken for the cuttings to root will depend on the kind of protection given, but can be as little as two weeks or may take two months or more. They should be potted up as soon as they are rooted, unless rooting takes place so late that winter has arrived, in which case it is better to delay until early spring. Semi-ripe cuttings are used for propagation more frequently than any other kind. There is, with most plants, plenty of leeway over the period when such cuttings will root.

Leaf-bud Cutting

This is a modification of the semi-ripe cutting, consisting of a single node—a portion of stem with a single leaf and axillary bud. This technique can be used when propagation material is scarce or where one does not wish to spoil the stock plant by taking off too much growth. Some plants that can be propagated by leaf-bud cuttings include *Hedera* species and cultivars, *Fuchsia* species and cultivars, *Mahonia* species and most species of *Sedum*.

Soft Cuttings

Soft cuttings are taken from growth outside from mid spring to early summer, usually in a period of no more than a month and for some plants half of this

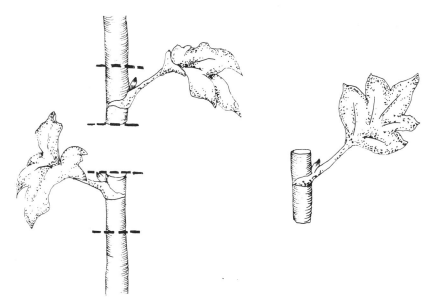

Figure 17   Leaf-bud cutting

31

period. Potted plants can provide suitable material over a longer period by bringing them into a warm glasshouse when dormant. When dormancy has resulted from drought, earlier watering may start the plant into new growth which will produce material suitable for making soft cuttings. Care should be taken with their handling, as these cuttings are soft and succulent and when pressed will squash, or if bent will snap. For successful rooting more sophisticated protection is needed: mist, closed case, propagator, or other sealed container. Hygiene is important at all stages of propagation, for the soft material is susceptible to infection by disease agents. Totally immersing cuttings after preparation in a solution of Captan or Benlate will provide protection. All unwanted plant material should be taken away from the place where cuttings are being propagated and any leaves on inserted cuttings showing infection should be removed. Soft cuttings root very quickly, and when provided with bottom heat this can be as short a time as seven days, although 10–14 is more usual. As soon as these cuttings are rooted they should be potted. Following potting the cuttings should be stood in a closed case until new growth begins, after which the humidity should be gradually reduced until the plants can be stood on an open bench. When bottom heat is available under mist, or a closed case or propagator is used, this means of propagation is more likely than other means to prove successful with plants that are normally difficult to root.

Preparation

Internodal cuttings are prepared by making a horizontal cut immediately above a single or pair of buds with a second cut 1–2in (25–50mm) below the node; the prepared cutting is inserted into the rooting medium so that the petiole(s) rest(s) on the surface. This method of propagation is used for *Clematis*, although a few other kinds of plants will root readily if prepared in this manner. The most usual is the nodal cutting, where the basal cut is made immediately below the nodes. With many alpine plants this is just above the point where new growth has commenced in the current season. Where growth is substantial, the basal cut will be about 2in (50mm) below the growing point. One or a few basal leaves will be removed, sufficient to allow insertion of cutting into the rooting medium. When stems have very short leaves, as with *Erica* species and cultivars, or where leaves are scale-like, as with *Helichrysum selago*, it is preferable not to remove the basal leaves.

It can be advantageous to take some cuttings with a heel—that is a portion of older wood from which current growth has arisen. Heel cuttings are preferable on plants that bleed, such as taxa of Aponcynaceae, some Compositae and Euphorbiaceae. It can also be beneficial with conifers where current growth when cut exudes resin. Cuttings of *Berberis* species and cultivars also seem to root better when they have a heel.

There can be improvement in rooting of some cuttings taken from woody plants if the base of the cutting is wounded. With some plants it may be enough to pull or rub off the leaves instead of removing with a knife, but it is more usual to take off a sliver of bark sufficient to expose the wood beneath. Wounding is beneficial on *Ilex crenata*, species of *Acer* and most conifers (*see* Fig. 19).

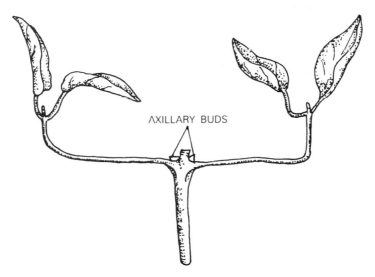

AXILLARY BUDS

Figure 18   Internodal cutting of Clematis

Rooting Hormones

When a piece of a living plant is removed, naturally occurring substances produced by the growing point are translocated to the cut end where cells are stimulated to produce a callus, which heals the wound and stimulates the formation of root initials. These substances have been isolated and these and related chemicals manufactured artificially. Called rooting hormones, these preparations when applied to the base of cuttings act in the same way as natural substances. The chemical most commonly used is IBA (Indol butyric acid), which is most usually offered for sale in powder form where the active ingredient has been mixed with talc. For the amateur there are three grades: no. 1 for soft cuttings, no. 2 for semi-ripe cuttings and no. 3 for hardwood. The effective life of these preparations is short, for the active ingredient breaks down in high temperatures and when exposed to light.

When not in use the tops of the storage containers should be screwed on tight and stored in a cool place. As a protection against disease agents infecting buried portions of cuttings, it can be advantageous to incorporate fungicide with the rooting powder, for example flowers-of-sulphur, Benlate or Captan. Experiments with Captan have suggested that it can stimulate root formation on cuttings. With the exception of woody plants, it is doubtful if rooting hormones have any beneficial effect on the rooting of cuttings of alpine plants.

33

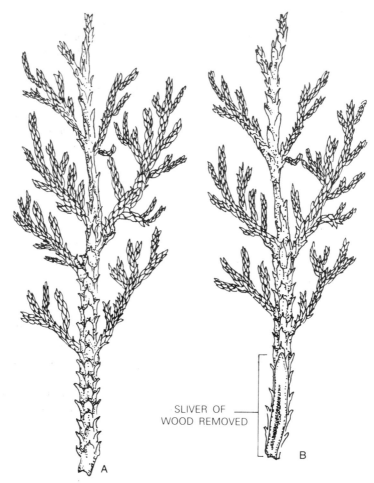

SLIVER OF
WOOD REMOVED

A

B

PREPARED CONIFER CUTTING

Figure 19   Wounding of cuttings

More benefit is likely if Captan is used as an alternative, since in addition to its fungicidal properties it stimulates rooting. There is, however, some benefit in using number 3 strength of hormone powder with woody cuttings that have been wounded.

The use of over-strength hormone powder can cause damage to the treated cuttings and can result in excessive callus production which inhibits emergence of roots. If ever there is excessive callus production resulting from hormone application, or even without, it should be broken off or cut away.

Whilst hormone application can be beneficial on stem cuttings, it should not be used on leaf-bud cuttings, for although it may speed up rooting it will inhibit axillary bud development. There is no advantage in its application to leaf or root cuttings (*see* Leaf Cuttings p 40 and Root Cuttings p 42).

34

Rooting Media

The material into which cuttings are inserted must support them, provide aeration, be water retentive, sterile and preferably have a pH below 7.

SAND is readily available almost anywhere, in packs at a garden centre or in larger loads from sandworks or quarries. It provides perfect drainage and good aeration but there is no water retention. The best type is a coarse grade with particle size between $\frac{1}{16}$ and $\frac{1}{4}$in (1–5 mm) and with a pH below 6.5. Avoid sand that is very fine, from the sea shore, alkaline or contains clay.

PERLITE is available from garden centres in packs of various sizes. This lightweight material with a pH of 6–6.5 provides good aeration and drainage but there is no water retention.

PUMICE is available in packs from many garden centres and may also occasionally be obtainable elsewhere. Select a grade of between $\frac{1}{16}$ and $\frac{1}{8}$in (1.5–3mm), which will provide excellent drainage and aeration even though there is little water retention; check the pH, which can be variable.

VERMICULITE is sometimes used as packing material but it also can be purchased at garden centres. This flaky material is light in weight, porous and water retentive; avoid grades that are too fine as drainage can be impaired.

PEAT which is water retentive has poor drainage and with fine grades there can be poor aeration. Sphagnum peat, which is the best, is available from all garden centres in packs of various sizes. Before use ensure that it is evenly moist, for dry peat is difficult to wet. Peat potting or seed composts are not suited for use in propagation.

BARK FIBRE is prepared from the outer bark of trees and is waste product of forestry. It has been pulverised so as to produce a range of grades and is sold partially decomposed. The price of loads is largely dependent on the distance from the source of supply, but packs are available from many garden centres. It has good aeration, is retentive of moisture and there is usually a pH below 7.

These materials can be used on their own, but peat and sand especially are more often mixed with other materials. Percentages of each in a mix can vary but 50/50 is the usual.

Protection

When leafy cuttings are removed from a plant they must be kept turgid at all times until rooted. To achieve this a high humidity has to be maintained by repeated watering and/or spraying over with water. Drying out can be reduced by enclosing the cuttings, reducing air movement and providing shading so that there is less transpiration in sunlight and its heat will not result in an increase of evaporation.

In the Home

The simplest method is to cover pots of cuttings with glass jars; an alternative is to cover with a polythene bag which is kept in place by an elastic band. Translucent food containers, such as those used for sandwiches, ice-creams or frozen food make ideal small propagators. Put 1in (25mm) of moist rooting medium into a clean container, insert the cuttings and replace the lid tightly; do not open until the cuttings have rooted. Larger numbers of cuttings can be rooted in a deep wooden box/flat that is covered with a sheet of glass or rigid clear plastic; another method is to staple on a sheet of taut polythene, or a plastic tray/flat can be put into a large polythene bag.

There are plant propagators of various sizes on the market. These consist of a basal tray for the rooting medium wth a clear plastic top. Additional modifications include bottom heat, thermostatic heating controls and self-watering devices. All these containers, which are easy to handle and to clean, can be positioned on window-sills or in porches. Expose to maximum light but provide protection from direct sun. As well as using these in the home they can be used within frames, tunnels or glasshouses.

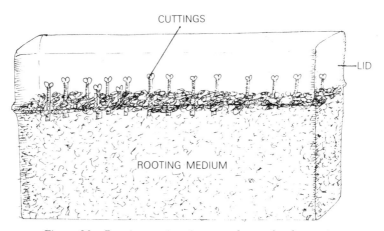

Figure 20   Rooting cuttings in a translucent food container

Frames

In the garden it is likely that frames will be most used for propagation. They may be intended solely for propagation when quantities of cuttings to be rooted are large, but they may also accommodate plants for growing on or be used for plant storage. Cuttings may be rooted in separate containers and stood on a porous substrate such as gravel, sand or ashes, or they can be plunged. An alternative is to make up beds of rooting medium within the frames into which the cuttings can be inserted.

The simplest frames are those made of baulks of timber, such as railway sleepers. More sophisticated ones can be made of wood, brick, breeze blocks or reinforced concrete. The backs of the frames should be higher than the front. Their depth will depend on the use of the frames and the size and kind of plant to be accommodated; 12in (300mm) at the back is a fair average. Frame tops will be covered with panes or sheets of glass, rigid clear plastic or taut polythene. It is better when the frame tops are provided with cross members to give support to the lights, to act as runners and prevent drips. If propagation is to be restricted to only part of the frame, it should be partitioned off. Established plants, those being grown under protection, specimen plants and those used for showing will need maximum ventilation throughout the year, with perhaps total removal during the summer. Lights over cuttings will need to be kept permanently closed to retain humidity. Sunlight will increase both evaporation and transpiration so that shading will become necessary at least in spring and summer. This can be with an application of a lime wash to the glass or plastic or by covering with sheets of a thin, fine plastic mesh; this has the advantage of being easily removed in dull weather.

Tunnels

These consist of sheets of polythene stretched over a series of metal hoops to make enclosed structures. The tunnels can be of varying heights from 1ft (30cm) to 6ft (2m) or even more. Temperatures inside the lowest types can be high in summer, when it is usual to open or roll up the sides. As this reduces the humidity, these low tunnels are most often used for autumn/fall rooting of cuttings or to provide winter protection for cuttings of hardy evergreens. By spring these will have rooted so that the opening of the tunnels poses no problems.

The largest tunnels can be walked into and may be a practical alternative to glasshouses. Indeed, because of their relative cheapness tunnels are now being used for commercial propagation as well as for plant cropping. It is not difficult nor unduly expensive for these structures to be provided with heating, but again summer heat can become excessive. In these larger structures there is far less loss of humidity if the sides are rolled up, and it is common practice to have strips of mesh along the base of the sides to improve ventilation without seriously reducing humidity. In fact, in colder periods improved air movement is beneficial. If it is very cold outside in winter, additional plastic can be let down over the ventilating mesh.

Hoops and polythene for low tunnels can be bought in special packs. It is also possible to buy these for the larger tunnels if you are a do-it-yourself addict, but they are better erected by professionals. The covering polythene is available in different thicknesses and quality; the milky kind is the best, as it obviates the need for shading. There is also treated polythene, which reduces condensation, although chemicals can be bought and sprayed on which will do the same job. All forms of polythene cladding have a limited life, for with continued exposure to sunlight they become brittle and crack or tear easily. Those kinds sold as UV (ultra-violet) resistant do not guarantee permanence, they simply extend the life by one or perhaps two years. The average lifespan of commercially-used polythene cladding is often only three years, but in amateur use it can last longer before replacement becomes necessary.

A large tunnel is unlikely to be used solely for propagation—benches can be installed which will enable easier handling of cuttings, the establishment of rooted cuttings, plant storage or protection of border-line hardy specimen plants. Frames can be introduced or propagating beds made up on the floor.

Glasshouses

These structures may have either wooden beams or glazing bars which go down to the ground or to a wooden or brick base. Glazing bars tend to be substantial, especially when supporting large panes of glass, which can reduce light admission. Wooden structures need to be painted or be treated periodically with oil. Aluminium structures are now more common. These allow narrower glazing bars, thus allowing maximum light to be admitted at all times. Furthermore, there is no maintenance needed with aluminium houses. Glasshouses can be heated, which may be automatically controlled, as can watering, damping, ventilation and even shading. Most houses can be provided with benches to maximise space and to improve working conditions.

Propagation can be carried out in pots, boxes/flats, propagators or frames inside the house. An alternative is to make up beds of rooting medium and insert prepared cuttings into these. The rooting of cuttings can be speeded up by providing these beds with heat from below.

Waterproofed heating cables are laid on a level bed of sand, covered with another layer to a depth of $\frac{1}{2}$in (12mm) onto which is placed 3–4in (75–100mm) of a rooting medium. The cables will be attached to a thermostat where a setting of 70°F (21°C) should be the maximum. Bottom heat in general is unnecessary for alpines but is beneficial for small shrubs and dwarf conifers; it can be provided for outside frames, within tunnels or under mist beds.

The most sophisticated propagation aid is a mist unit where it is possible to have absolute control over humidity. At the bottom of the bed are horizontal water pipes from which there are verticals with mist nozzles. The water supply is controlled by a solenoid valve activated by an electronic leaf which is positioned amongst the cuttings. If the surface of this electronic leaf is covered with a film of water the valve remains closed. However, when the moisture has all evaporated, the contact between the electrodes is broken and mist comes on. The horizontal water pipes are covered with sand on which heating cables are laid to provide bottom heat to warm the rooting medium which will be 3–4in (75–100mm) deep.

For an alpine gardener the greatest benefit from a mist unit is in the rooting of soft cuttings and those which are known to be difficult to root.

38

Establishment

Rooting of cuttings is only part of plant propagation, even though it may be the most important aspect; rooted cuttings have then to be established in containers of compost. Cuttings rooted under mist or other enclosed protection where there is a high humidity need to be acclimatised to the lower humidity of an open bench or frame. With a mist unit, reduce the frequency of misting a little at a time; open closed frames or propagators for increasing periods and remove glass jars, polythene bags and sheets of glass, plastic or polythene.

Rooted cuttings will be transferred singly to separate containers. These can be plastic or clay pots which will vary between 2 and 4in (50–100mm) in diameter: the smallest will be for weak or slow growers or where cuttings are poorly rooted, whilst the largest are for the strongest growers; take care not to overpot, otherwise watering during establishment will be difficult. Peat pots or peat blocks are alternatives, but after potting these should be packed into boxes/flats as an aid for when they have to be moved. Plants in peat containers need to be planted out or potted on as soon as roots emerge. There are paper, composition and waxed cardboard pots, whilst drinking cups of paper, plastic or polystyrene can be used as long as they are clean and provided with drainage holes.

There is a wide range of potting composts available from garden centres, but trial and error or shopping around may be necessary to find one which is suitable and reliable. Composts based solely on peat can be used for strong growers or when plants are to be in containers for no more than weeks or a few months. Peat composts are not suited to plants which are to overwinter in their pots, especially if these are plunged outside. Bark fibres or even peat, with sand, are suitable for overwintering plants but the ideal are those which are soil based. The best are those prepared to the formula of John Innes Potting Compost.

If a suitable soil-based compost cannot be found the following recipe will produce an ideal potting compost:

3 parts sterilised soil
2 parts peat
1 part sharp sand
(all parts by volume).

It is desirable to know the pH of the soil. An acid soil where the pH is below 7 is suited to a wide range of plants including lime lovers, although the latter will benefit from the addition of lime in the form of ground limestone or hydrated lime. For lime lovers it may be preferable to replace totally or in part the sand with limestone chips. A sprinkling of bonemeal will provide added nutrients, as will a suitable number of ground tablets manufactured for the feeding of houseplants. It may be desirable to amend this recipe by increasing the peat or the sand.

Ericaceae will benefit from a more organic soil:

1 part sterilised lime-free soil
1 part peat
1 part sharp sand
(all parts by volume).

Rooting media contain no plant nutrients and if cuttings are left alone once rooted, they will quickly starve. Cuttings should be potted as soon as they have rooted, which offers no problems in summer or autumn/fall or when there is heated protection. In areas with a cold winter, if cuttings root late in cold frames, unheated glasshouses or tunnels, it is better to delay potting until the following spring just prior to new growth. Having reduced humidity, rooted cuttings should be lifted carefully with a handfork from bed, box, tray or flat. Cuttings rooted in pots should be watered before being knocked out, when they need careful separation.

Put a small amount of potting compost into the bottom of the pot; hold the rooted cutting in the centre high enough so that leaves will not be buried and with the other hand overfill; tap and firm with the fingers. Watering will be with a rosed can which will settle the compost. A second watering should not be given until the compost has almost dried out. Continue this careful watering; too much water at this stage produces a cold compost with poor aeration. Ensure there is a label with each batch of plants, although it is desirable that there is a label in each pot. Following potting, keep under protection, shading if necessary, until plants are established and beginning to grow away. At this stage they should be transferred to a plunge bed or cold frame.

Potted rooted cuttings of some deciduous subjects, for example *Rhododendron*, *Daphne* and *Clematis*, need to produce secondary growth before leaf fall otherwise they seldom survive the winter. Following potting, they should be kept in a glasshouse or tunnel, perhaps in a closed frame or under a polythene cover so as to encourage secondary growth. If these cuttings are not rooted before autumn/fall, do not disturb until the following spring.

Care should be taken to ensure that the compost in which these plants are growing is kept uniformly moist. Once established they can be watered by can without a rose, or by hosepipe. Take preventative measures against fungal diseases or pests by regular sprayings; put down pellets to combat slugs and snails. Protection against root aphids or vine weevil larvae is by adding lindane dust to the potting compost. Plant out or pot on before the plant becomes rootbound.

Leaf Cuttings

A leaf cutting consists of a length of petiole and the lamina only. As there is no bud, the leaf must be capable of producing adventitious roots and adventitious buds. This method of propagation is mostly used with plants that belong to the family *Gesneriaceae*. Plants with variegated foliage are not suitable for propagation by leaf cuttings.

Whilst success can be achieved with leaves of any age and condition, the best results are from new fully mature leaves. With rosette-formers, the soil should be scraped away from around the base of the plant so that the points of origin of the leaves can be seen. Leaves should be detached carefully from the outside of the rosette so that the petiole comes away in its entirety. These detached leaves are inserted into rooting medium around the edge of a small pot; a clay pot gives better and quicker results than one made of plastic. Insert the petiole only deep enough so that when the cuttings are firmed they will stand upright. The containers can be protected by plastic or placed within a frame, closed case or on a glasshouse bench.

The more warmth that can be provided, the quicker will be the rooting and the production of a new plant. First to appear will be roots from the base of the petiole followed later by a bud just above. The length of time before this bud produces leaves and a plantlet appears above the surface of the rooting medium will be determined by the depth of insertion of the petiole. *Conandron ramondioides* is a Gesneriad which is herbaceous and in autumn/fall the leaf dies away to a resting tuber. If this species is being propagated by leaves without heat, the leaf may die away before a plantlet has appeared above ground. If this happens, keep the pot, reduce water and provide winter protection and the new plant will appear in the following spring.

This method of propagation is effective with many species within the petiolarid group of *Primula*. In *Tolmiea menziesii* a plantlet will develop where

Prepared leaf cutting

Cuttings inserted around edge of pot

Figure 21   Leaf cuttings

41

PLANTLET

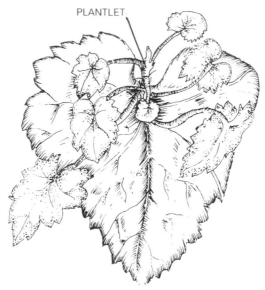

Figure 22 Tolmiea menziesii

the petiole joins the lamina. Detach the leaf with a portion of petiole, fold back the lamina and cover it with rooting medium so that the plantlet protrudes.

Although most species of *Begonia* are warm glasshouse plants, a few small ones are suitable for cultivation on the rock garden of which *B. evansii* is the best known. Trays or flats are better than pots for the rooting of Begonia leaves. Loosely fill these with rooting medium; firm and level and cover with a thin layer of sand. Detach fully developed new leaves with a short length of petiole and cut through the thickest veins on the undersurface. Using a dibber insert the petiole so that the lamina lies flat on the surface of the rooting medium; keep this in close contact by putting pebbles onto the leaf surface. Cover the container with a sheet of glass or polythene. The first plantlet to appear is usually at the point where the lamina joins the petiole; with luck the cut veins will also produce plantlets. Some ferns can be propagated by leaf cuttings treated in this manner.

Root Cuttings

As less research has been carried out with this method of propagation, it is probably that many more plants can be increased by this means than is generally thought. This method must not be used to increase grafted plants or those which have variegated foliage. For plants to be able to be increased by root cuttings, roots must be capable of producing both adventitious buds and adventitious roots. The time of the year when these cuttings respond best is soon after the stock plant has gone dormant. With woody plants this is usually' in early winter but with plants such as *Primula denticulata* it is early summer soon after flowering is over.

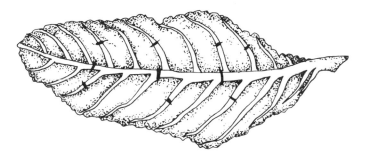

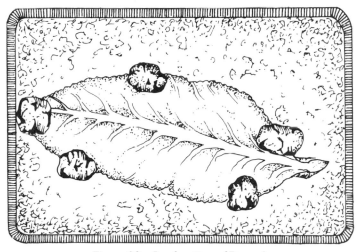

Figure 23   Leaf cutting of Begonia

The plant to be propagated should be lifted carefully, shaken and the soil washed off the roots. Take off some of the thickest roots leaving enough of the root system to allow establishment of the stock plant after replanting. The detached roots are cut into pieces of 1–2in (25–50mm) and if there are fibrous roots attached these are trimmed. A box/flat is partially filled with a potting compost, firmed and levelled and then covered with a layer of rooting medium about ½in (12mm) deep. The portions of root are scattered over the firmed, level surface of the rooting medium, pressed into it and just covered with more rooting medium (*see* Figs 24 & 25).

Where roots are more substantial, say approaching the thickness of a pencil, there is a different technique, as with *Morisia monanthos*. Cut the root into pieces about 1in (25mm) in length, making a flat cut at the proximal end (that nearest to the stem) and a sloping cut at the distal end (that furthest from the stem). These cuttings are inserted vertically into tray/flats or pots of rooting medium, pointed end downwards and with the flat top just below the surface of the rooting medium that covers them. Keep the rooting medium moist without being excessively wet and provide some protection without heat (*see* Fig. 26).

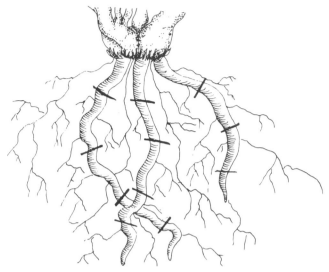

Figure 24   Primula denticulata, *showing cuts on thicker roots*

Sometimes when potted plants have been plunged roots grow through the drainage holes into the plunge material. When the pots are being moved these roots break off and the buried portion will act as a root cutting, and as long as not buried too deeply will eventually produce a new plant, as will occur with *Matthiola fruticulosa*.

Layering

Layering should be practised when propagation by cuttings is difficult or impossible. It can be complementary to cuttings, for it is easy to layer single plants in the rock garden but large numbers are unsightly and inconvenient. Too many container-grown plants which are layered can be a nuisance as they are difficult to handle. The aim in layering is to encourage a stem to produce

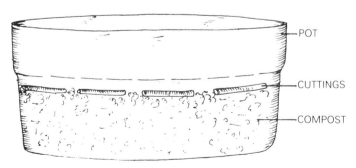

Figure 25   Root cuttings 'sown' on rooting medium

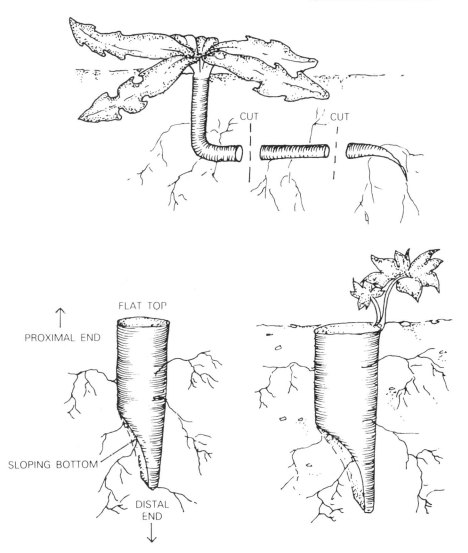

Figure 26   Preparation of thicker root cuttings

adventitious roots whilst attached to its parent. Although rooting of layers can be a slow process, from five to 24 months, the parent provides food materials over this lengthy period.

Layering is better suited to low-growing and prostrate plants than to upright plants. As with cuttings, the best results will be obtained from young parent plants. The stems to be used for layering should be of the current season's growth, for although older wood can be induced to root this can be a lengthy process, with fewer roots on the new plant, which may be difficult to establish. Some hard pruning in the season before layering is to be carried out is desirable

45

so as to produce strong young shoots from ground level. Stems for layering need to be supple so that they bend easily without breaking. The best seasons are early spring before new growth begins or later summer–early autumn/fall after new growth is complete. Early spring is better for deciduous subjects and should be used for plants growing in gardens where summer and autumn/fall can be dry; but it is the suppleness of the stems that must be the deciding factor.

For layering a sharp knife is needed, a supply of pegs and perhaps tying material and garden canes. Pegs are made from a heavy gauge wire which is bent into a U shape resembling a large staple 2–4in (50–100mm) long. Take out a slit trench 4–6in (100–150mm) deep and half fill with a mixture of equal parts peat and sand. The stem to be layered is then bent until it is U-shaped and pushed into the trench where it is secured with the peg at the lowest part of the U. The soil should then be pushed back into the trench and firmed with the heel, pulling the tip of the shoot upright. It may also be necessary to secure it to a cane to ensure that it remains upright. Leaves on portions of stem that will be below ground should be removed before layering. It is beneficial to restrict the stem at its lowest portion by one of the following means: tying a piece of copper wire tightly around the stem; taking off a sliver of bark sufficient to expose the wood on the underside of the stem; removing a strip of bark $\frac{1}{4}$–$\frac{1}{2}$in (5–10mm) wide around the stem; or making a tongue of $\frac{1}{2}$–$\frac{3}{4}$in (10–15mm). Areas which have been cut can be rubbed with hormone powder no. 3.

Subsequent treatment is to ensure that the soil remains moist, and in a dry summer and autumn/fall regular irrigation is desirable. The length of time it will take for a layer to produce roots will vary from species to species, genus to genus and even cultivar to cultivar. Rhododendrons usually take the longest— from 18 months to two years. With other plants rooting may be adequate by early spring of the following year. Early spring, just prior to the commencement of new shoot growth, is the best time to lift rooted layers. These can be potted, lined out in a nursery or planted directly onto the rock garden.

With some woody prostrate plants, it may be enough to remove a sliver of bark to expose the wood on the undersurface of a stem in contact with the soil and hold it in position by stone or peg. Some low-growing plants, such as *Abeliophyllum distichum*, produce stems which come down to the ground where they will root naturally; holding these down so they remain in contact with the soil by using a stone or peg will be an aid.

An easier way to treat perennials is by putting a spadeful of a mixture of peat and sand into the centre of a clump and working it in between the stem bases; leaves should be removed rather than buried. This method can also be effective with some woody plants such as *Erica* species and cultivars that produce many short stems from ground level (*see* Figs 27 & 28).

Grafting

Grafting defines the operation where parts of two different plants are brought together so that the tissues of both unite to form a single new plant. There are

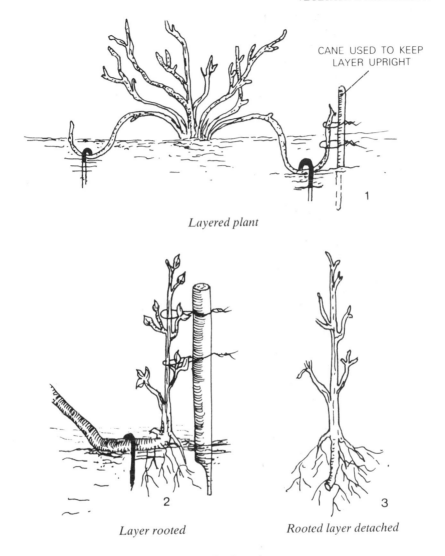

CANE USED TO KEEP
LAYER UPRIGHT

1

Layered plant

2

Layer rooted

3

Rooted layer detached

Figure 27   Layering

two parts to a graft: stock (a contraction of understock or rootstock), which will be the root system, and scion, which will become the aerial part of the new plant. For a successful union stock and scion must be compatible, there must be skilled knifemanship so that the cut surfaces are in intimate contact and the cambium layers in both are lined up, and there must be good after care.

Compatibility refers to the relationship or botanical affinity between stock and scion. There will be compatibility between a cultivar and the species of which it is a selection: for example *Cryptomeria japonica* 'Spiralis' can be grafted successfully onto *C. japonica* seedlings. Equally there will be success

47

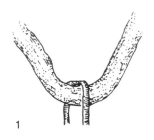
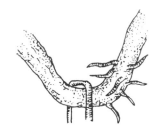

1

AFTER MAKING CUT
THE STEM IS TWISTED

2

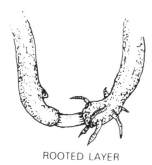

TONGUE NOW
DOWNWARD POINTING

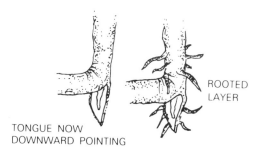

ROOTED
LAYER

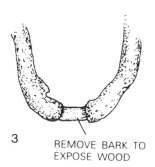

REMOVE BARK TO
EXPOSE WOOD

3

ROOTED LAYER

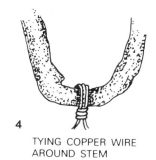

TYING COPPER WIRE
AROUND STEM

4

ROOTED LAYER

Figure 28   Layering methods

amongst cultivars of the same species, so that if a gardener has surplus plants of say, *C.j.* 'Elegans' they will be suitable stocks for *Spiralis* cultivars. Compatibility is usual between different species and their cultivars within the same genus: for example *Rhododendron ponticum* is the commonest nursery stock used in the propagation of different species, cultivars and hybrids.

There can be exceptions, especially in genera which have large numbers of species such as *Prunus, Acer* and *Rhododendron*. For example, Victoria plum, which is a cultivar of *Prunus domestica*, is incompatible with seedling sour cherry, *Prunus cerasus*. Snake bark maples (species of *Acer* with striated bark) are incompatible with the common sycamore, *Acer pseudoplatanus*, which is the usual *Acer* stock used in nurseries. Even in the genus *Rhododendron*, which has some 800 species, there can be incompatibility with *R. ponticum*. It cannot be used as a stock for deciduous azaleas. There can also be compatibility between some genera in the same family. Eating pears, cultivars of *Pyrus domestica*, are grafted commercially onto common quince, *Cydonia oblonga*. In the past it was normal practice for nurserymen to use common privet, *Ligustrum vulgare*, as a stock for cultivars of the common lilac, *Syringa vulgaris*.

If the gardener is able to choose a rootstock for a plant to be propagated, s/he should try to use the same species of which it is a selection. If this is not possible, as with a cultivar of a rare species, a different species in the same genus should be selected. In large genera, such as *Rhododendron*, a species in the same series should be chosen, and with *Prunus* one from the same group. When species in the same genus are not available, one in a closely allied genus may be used, but be prepared for failure.

Occasionally a gardener will have surplus plants of suitable size established in pots and which are compatible. Most often the gardener wil have to raise his or her own stocks. Seedling stock is to be preferred, for there is less chance that this will be infected with virus. Following sowing, the seedlings should be potted singly into small pots of say 3½in (90mm). The seedlings must be grown on until there is a good root system and a thickness of basal stem of at least ¼in (5mm). Rootstocks can be raised from cuttings as long as the stock plant is healthy, and this will usually produce a suitable plant for grafting in fewer years.

Characteristics of a rootstock, such as pest and disease resistance, habit and ultimate size can be transferred to a scion. Merton/Malling apple rootstocks are resistant to woolly aphis (*Eriosoma lanigerum*), a pest with a waxy white woolly covering that affects twigs and young branches; it passes this resistance to cultivars that are grafted onto it. The sweet cherry rootstock 12/1 passes its resistance to bacterial canker (*Pseudomonas mors-prunorum*) on to its grafted cultivars. Pear trees when growing on their own roots or grafted onto seedling pears produce trees of 15ft (5m), whereas if grafted onto common quince they produce bushes of about 9ft (3m).

The selection of stocks for dwarf conifers or dwarf rhododendrons is important, otherwise an over-large bush completely out of character may

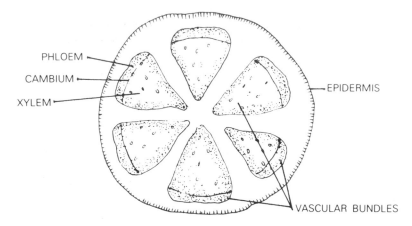

PHLOEM

CAMBIUM

XYLEM

EPIDERMIS

VASCULAR BUNDLES

Figure 29   Cross section of a dicot stem

result. Grafting as a means of propagation should be used only when all other methods are unsuccessful.

It is essential when joining scion to stock that the cambium layers are lined up. This is because within the stem of a plant there are vascular bundles that act as conducting channels. Their inner cells form xylem, or wood, which carries water and dissolved mineral nutrients from the roots to leaves. The outer cells form phloem, which transports manufactured food materials from leaves to roots. Xylem and phloem are separated in dicotyledonous plants by the cambium, which is a single layer of meristematic cells. When a stem is cut, the cambium will produce a callus to seal the wound. In a graft, the cambium in the stock and scion produces new xylem and phloem cells so that the vascular bundles of each unite and the cut surfaces are then sealed with a callus.

Materials required for grafting are: compatible rootstocks established in $3\frac{1}{2}$in (90mm) pots, secateurs, a sharp knife or scalpel and tying materials. The most usual time for grafting is late winter or early spring whilst both stock and scion are dormant; sometimes grafting can be carried out in late summer or early autumn/fall after the current season's growth is complete. Skill is needed in the use of a knife so that all cuts are smooth and even and both stock and scion fit closely together. Before carrying out the operation on the chosen plant, practice cuts should be made on thin woody prunings until the technique is mastered.

For best results, the stock should be starting into growth whilst the scion remains dormant. Pot-grown stocks are brought into gentle warmth in late winter. Apply only enough water to the pots to ensure the compost is just moist. As soon as new root growth has commenced, grafting can take place. Scion material is collected from the rock garden or potted specimen plants. With those that start early into growth and with protected pot plants, scion material should be collected in mid-winter whilst absolutely dormant and stored in polythene bags in a refrigerator or heeled in in the coldest part of the garden. Take off almost the whole of the current season's side growth of all plants except those conifers with a tiered habit such as *Abies, Cedrus, Picea* and *Pinus* where only terminal shoots should be taken.

There are perhaps more than a hundred different kinds of grafts, but I am going to mention only two, which in my opinion are the easiest: cleft and side grafts.

Cleft Graft
Remove the top of the rootstock with secateurs with clean, sharp cutting blades at 1–2in (25–50mm) above pot level. Make a downward cut across the diameter of the rootstock ½–¾in (12–19mm) deep using a sharp knife of scalpel. The length of the scion will vary with the kind of plant and the amount of current season's growth and can be 1–2in (25–50mm) long; it is usual to remove the apical bud. At the base of the scion make an even wedge, the sloping sides of which measure ½–¾in (12–19mm). Exercise strict control with the knife or scalpel so that cuts are smooth and even. With the tip of the knife/scalpel open up the cut on the stock and insert the wedge of the scion, line up the cambiums

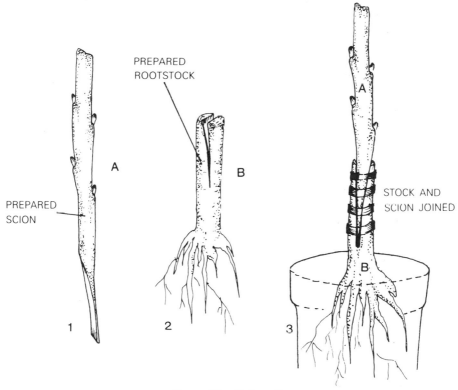

Figure 30   Cleft graft

51

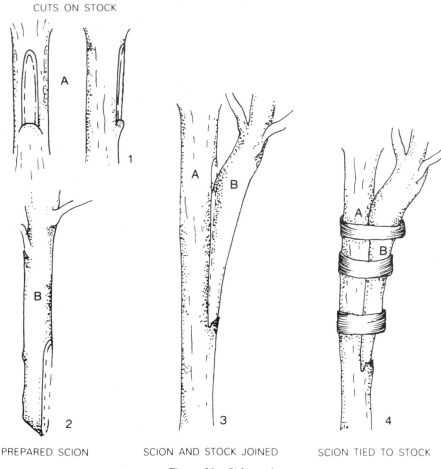

CUTS ON STOCK

PREPARED SCION   SCION AND STOCK JOINED   SCION TIED TO STOCK

Figure 31   Side graft

and remove the knife/scalpel. The springiness of the wood should hold the scion firmly in position. Even so, wrapping tying material around the cut on the stock will ensure that cut surfaces remain in tight contact.

Side Graft

Make the first $\frac{1}{4}$in (6mm) cut on the stock about 1in (25mm) above pot level at an angle of 30°, then remove the blade of the cutting instrument. A second cut should begin $\frac{1}{2}$–1in (12–25mm) above the first and travel downwards at a slight angle until the two meet; remove the resulting sliver. With conifers or evergreens, any leaves should be rubbed off the lowest 3in (75mm) of the stock before making any cuts. In preparation of the scion, the growing point is removed for deciduous and evergreen subjects but retained for conifers. With evergreen scions, remove the lowest leaves with a sharp knife/scalpel so that they do not interfere with the grafting cuts. Conifers must also have the needles removed from the base of the scion; the distance from the base that these must be removed will be dictated by the length of the grafting cuts to be made, but rather more may have to be removed on conifers where long needles will interfere with subsequent tying.

At the base of the scion make an even-sloping cut to correspond in length to the longest on the stock; reverse and make a second cut an ⅛–¼in (3–6mm) so as to form an uneven wedge (see figures). Join the long cut to the scion so that the cambiums on one side at least are joined up. Push downwards so that the wedge tip of the scion sits on or is held by the lip of the cut on the stock; then tie securely to hold the scion firmly in position. Fold the tie material so that at least ¾in (18mm) points upwards against the stock and then tie over it. Leave space between the different strands so that the stock can be seen; finally, secure with a half-hitch.

Following grafting it is necessary to keep plants in a humid place. Cover with large glass jars, polythene bags or keep plunged in a closed case. When covered by a glass jar or polythene bag the plants should be double potted. Take a larger sized empty pot and put into it a small amount of sand, place the base of the potted stock onto it so that the upper levels of each are the same then pack more sand into the space between. Within all the enclosed areas of the covered grafts, loss of water by transpiration or evaporation will thus be minimal.

If there is any drying out, water only the plunge material or the sand in double-potted plants. Warmth will aid healing of cut surfaces, but avoid too much otherwise the scion may start into growth too early, when the graft often fails. After four weeks callusing should be noticeable. Prop up glass jars and

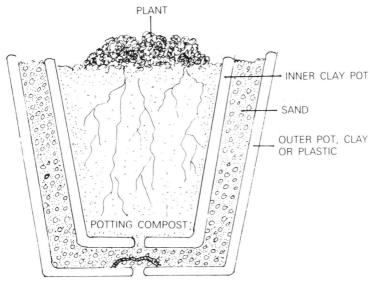

PLANT

INNER CLAY POT

SAND

OUTER POT, CLAY OR PLASTIC

POTTING COMPOST

Figure 32   Double potting

open polythene bags or closed frames so as to reduce humidity. As new shoots begin to develop on the scion, ordinary watering can begin. After about eight weeks, when the union is complete, the ties should be cut away and the length of stock above a side graft reduced by half. When it is obvious that the graft has been successful the plant should be transferred outside to a frame. Any shoot growth that has developed on the rootstock is best left, although if it is unduly long it should be pinched back. In autumn/fall, when current growth of both stock and scion is complete, all the rootstock above a side graft can be removed as can any other shoots that have been produced on the stock.

3   Special Techniques

Bulbs

Bulbous plants have swollen subterranean storage organs that allow plants to remain dormant during adverse climatic conditions such as drought, cold or a combination of both, and to grow away rapidly when conditions are again favourable. Those regions of the world with a Mediterranean climate, where there is winter rain and summer drought, are rich in bulbs. Growth begins with the arrival of autumnal/fall rains followed by winter or spring flowering. Whilst aerial growth is taking place, underground new bulbs are being produced or existing ones extended. When summer arrives, seed pods are ripening and foliage is starting to die away whilst food materials are being drawn back into the bulb. In some plants, such as *Allium, Brodiaea, Calochortus* and many kinds of terrestrial orchids, foliage can begin to die as flower buds are developing. After seeds have been shed, although bulbs are externally dor mant, changes are taking place within and next season's flowers are being formed. Summer soil temperatures can be critical for flower-bud initiation. Bulbs originating from regions that have high summer temperatures may not flower, or do so only sporadically, in gardens where summers are cool or temperatures are low, as can happen in a permanently wet soil. In regions that experience summer rainfall and winter drought, growth takes place in summer.

When growing in woodland conditions, bulbs can provide a surge of growth so that flowering can take place before a new foliar canopy shuts out light and reduces rain penetration; soil of a woodland floor can be dry during summer and early autumn/fall. This surge of energy is also beneficial in allowing stems to get up above surrounding evergreen or herbaceous perennials. Summer soil temperatures are not so critical for flower-bud initiation in woodland bulbs.

With some bulbs, roots may die away completely along with aerial growth, as happens with *Narcissus, Crocus* and *Anemone*; these bulbs can be out of the ground for long periods when dormant without deterioration. In others, roots are perennial and need protection from drying out when lifted, for example *Cyclamen, Lilium* and *Nerine*. If these perennial roots are allowed to die, it seriously checks subsequent growth. Bulbs may make poor growth until new roots have been produced, they can remain dormant for a year or die completely. If foliage is damaged during the growing season by winter or spring frosts, other adverse climatic conditions, pests or diseases or incorrect cultivation, it can adversely affect flowering in subsequent years.

Bulbs bought from nurseries or garden centres may bloom well in the season following planting, but flowering may be poor in subsequent years. Conversely, some newly purchased bulbs following planting may languish for a year or two until they have fully established before they settle down and start flowering freely. Some bulbs such as tulips, hyacinths and *Camassia* species benefit from being lifted following flowering and stored in an airy shed until their foliage has died back. Being exposed to higher temperatures whilst out of the soil results in regular flowering following replanting which does not occur with permanent planting.

Bulbs in a Rock Garden

For centuries, bulbs have provided favourite garden plants in Europe. In their dormant state they could be out of the ground for long periods without deterioration and yet grow away when replanted, and this was an important consideration in days when transport was slow. Quick to bloom, flowers are brightly coloured and there is great diversity of form. This enthusiasim for bulbs has always been with rock gardeners, who have concentrated on the smaller kinds. Certain factors can affect the choice of suitable subjects for the rock garden. Some, as with particular species of *Allium* or *Muscari*, can be invasive and become weeds; others need lifting annually because they are tender or will not flower regularly when permanently planted (for instance *Ixia* and *Tulipa*).

More important—and a complaint that can be levelled against all bulbs—is that they can be dormant, in growth, in flower and die back at different times. Unless their position is clearly marked when dormant, there is the danger of replanting in an apparently empty pocket. Most unsatisfactory, though, is the untidy appearance of dying foliage. Whilst this can be hidden by planting under or through low-growing perennials, care must be taken to avoid ground cover with dense foliage, which insulates the soil against summer warmth, or strong growers with solid or invasive root systems that compete for soil moisture and nutrients.

Bulb Borders

A narrow border, perhaps 3ft (1m) wide at the base of a sunny wall can be used solely to accommodate bulbs. Such a wall will reflect the heat of the sun so that there is a microclimate where the temperature is always a few degrees higher than the open garden. Some heat will be absorbed by day to be released at night, which is beneficial in winter months to reduce frost penetration and provide protection to living leaves or precocious flowers. A wall sheds rain so that the soil at its base remains relatively dry. Increased heat and drier soil are conditions which are beneficial to ripening dormant bulbs.

Raised Beds

Specially prepared for plants that require perfect drainage, raised beds are well suited to more mature gardeners who find stooping difficult. Perfect surface drainage provides for a drier, warmer summer soil, which is advantageous to bulb ripening. Because of the spartan diet of a raised bed, some feeding may be necessary to ensure bulb increase.

Peat Gardens

Some bulbs prefer growing in an organic soil which remains moist throughout the year and which is cool during the summer months. Small bulbs that occur naturally in woodland, mountain moorlands or along stream sides can be grown here: for examples *Nomocharis*, *Trillium*, *Paris* and many species of *Fritillaria*.

Woodland

Taller-growing bulbs as well as some smaller ones that benefit from shady and cool soil conditions will grow successfully as long as the tree canopy is not too dense. In a small garden such conditions can be found in a border of shrubs provided that these are not closely planted and there is no mass of fibrous roots close to the surface. Suitable bulbs here are *Arisaema*, *Erythronium* and *Lilium*.

Bulbs in Containers

Bulbs in pots or pans are the easiest to handle. If kept under protection of frames, tunnels or glasshouses, it is possible to have complete control of watering; in summer there is improved ripening and there is winter protection of foliage and precocious flowers. The bulbs need only to be on display when in flower so that when foliage is dying back they do not distract and untidy leaves can be hidden away.

Large bulbs can be grown one to a pot, with the long tom (an extra deep pot) being the best. When the seedling bulb is put into the pot, only the roots will be covered by compost. In subsequent pottings, half of the height of the bulb will be exposed.

Smaller bulbs are better in pans, but when these are not available use half pots or fill a third of an ordinary pot with drainage material. In potting or repotting the bulbs will be just below the surface of the compost. Bulbs grow and flower better when root-bound. Potting on into larger pots should not be an annual event but should take place only when absolutely necessary. Even though they will not need to be potted on, they need handling annually.

When dormant, the single bulb should be removed from its pot with roots undisturbed, the hole checked for impeded drainage and the top inch (25mm) of compost replaced with new. Wait until smaller bulbs are completely dormant and the roots have died away completely. Remove them from their pan and grade them, separating the larger flowering sizes from the rest and repot these separately. Bulbs that have perennial roots should be removed from their pan, drainage checked, then returned to their pots and the top inch

(25mm) of compost replaced with new. Following potting, a decision has to be made as to when to begin watering. This will depend upon whether repotting is carried out immediately following dormancy or prior to new growth. With a large collection, it will take place over many weeks and bulbs can range between these two extremes. Often containers are watered immediately after repotting to settle the soil. A second watering should not take place until it can be seen that the soil has dried out; subsequent waterings will depend on need and external temperatures. It can be beneficial to withhold water in order to discourage precocious growth, which would be liable to damage by winter cold, for example in the Juno group of *Iris*.

Once the bulbs are growing strongly and have filled their pan with roots, feeding is beneficial. A liquid feed should be applied at two-weekly intervals until flower buds can be seen.

When flowering is over watering should be reduced. Far too many books advise gardeners to cease watering completely, with the explanation that soil dryness is essential for flower-bud initiation. This single fact is responsible for most deaths of bulbs in cultivation because the advice is taken literally. Whereas a dry soil is warmer than a wet one, it is soil temperature that is critical. If bulbs with perennial roots are kept so dry that these die, some bulbs can receive a check from which they may not recover, for example *Cyclamen*, *Nerine* and Oncocyclus *Iris*. All bulb containers benefit from being plunged, which reduces excessive drying out. In summer it can be beneficial to water the plunge material, as the porous nature of clay pots allows water to be absorbed from the plunge material. Individual plants can be double potted, and again if the sand between the two pots is watered, moisture can be absorbed through the clay pot.

For bulbs growing in plastic containers the compost should never be allowed to become dust dry, and water should be applied occasionally to prevent this happening.

Bulb Beds

Whilst there are many benefits from containerisation of most kinds of bulb, there are some limitations. When raised from seed, bulbs take many more years to reach flowering; bulb increase in pots is slower; there is greater loss of soil nutrient from more frequent watering of pots; there is less control of moisture availability to dormant bulbs in pots, whilst some, such as Juno and Oncocyclus *Iris*, grow better in beds than in pots. Permanent planting in beds can overcome these problems, maintenance is easier and bulbs can be left unattended.

Beds can be at ground level or raised by building walls of stone, brick, breeze blocks, reinforced concrete or timber, such as railway sleepers. Whether at ground level or raised, beds need to be covered by lights, high-standing frames, tunnels or glasshouses. Ensure that there is enough space between soil level and the glass to clear the tallest plant likely to be grown. For beds at ground level, excavate to a depth of 1ft (300mm) and put into the trench 4in (100mm) of drainage material, grading it from the coarsest at the bottom to the finest on top, using broken bricks, stone or clay pots, pebbles or gravel. The amount of drainage material for a raised bed will depend on the height of its sides and the kind of protection to be provided; built up to allow 6–8in (150–200mm) depth of compost. Cover the drainage material with a single layer of inverted turves that will prevent soil washing down and impeding drainage.

It is necessary to restrict bulbs that are growing in beds. Some kinds can run horizontally and appear amongst neighbours, causing mixing and resulting in competition. Bulbs will always find their own depth by working their way downwards naturally; at lifting these can sometimes be so deep that there is a chance of damage and adjacent clumps are disturbed.

In beds the drainage material level will stop bulbs working their way down lower, but there is need to control sideways spread. Make a series of enclosures 6in (150mm) square using brick, slate, wood or metal strips. Open square containers can be stitched together from plastic shading mesh or lattice pots can be packed tightly together. Fill the compartments/containers with a well-drained compost such as equal parts of sterilised loam, coarse sand and either peat or sterilised leaf mould. This recipe can be modified by altering the percentage of any of these ingredients. Apply to this mixture a dressing of bonemeal and a general or slow-release fertiliser. Most bulbs seem to prefer a neutral or alkaline soil, so apply a dressing of hydrated lime, ground limestone, limestone chips or magnesian limestone. When bulbs are known to be lime haters, no lime should be added and a lime-free loam should be chosen for the compost. Isolate the lime lovers and lime haters. Keep together the kinds that require the same treatment and that will be dormant together so as to simplify watering and feeding.

Before the initial planting, thoroughly soak the bed. Planting is best carried out in autumn/fall, although with bulbs which flower at that season, late summer is better. Whatever form of protection is provided, there must be maximum air movement at all times. Ventilators of a glasshouse should be fully open at all times and closed only in windy weather or if there is fog or frost. In some high-standing frames the sides will slide open or the glass can be taken out during the summer so that there is overhead protection from rain but maximum ventilation. Tunnels should have their sides rolled up and ends open at all times, being closed only when there are hard frosts. Because plastic traps and holds moisture, it can be beneficial to intall fans to move the air when stagnant conditions occur. Lights should be propped open and closed only when frosts or fog are forecast.

Seed sowing

Seeds of bulbous plants can be sown in pots of between 3 and 5in (75–125mm) in diameter, using a soil-based seed compost: fill, firm and produce a level surface and then sow very thinly. It is preferable to use several pots for a single batch of seed rather than crowd too many into a single pot. As the seed of many types of bulb is quite large, it is better to space-sow with from five to 20 per pot, depending on the kind of seed and size of pot. Following germination, seedlings should be watered for as long as they remain green. With many, seedlings will start to yellow and their tops will die away to leave minuscule bulblets. If this yellowing begins, reduce water and keep the compost drier, but at no time must it be allowed to become dust dry. With the tiniest seedlings or where only some seed has germinated, it is preferable to keep them in the same container for another year. Begin watering in autumn/fall as new roots begin to appear on the bulblets. The strongest seedlings will need to be potted singly into the smallest sized pots using a soil-based compost; carry out the potting as new root growth commences and just cover the bulblet. Water carefully and allow the soil to dry out before the next watering. Until there is a well-developed root system, careful watering is needed to avoid a permanently wet and cold compost that may be badly aerated. Again, keep the seedlings watered and growing until they start to yellow, when water should be reduced. In subsequent years feeding can be carried out at two-weekly intervals once there is a good root system, using a concentration of liquid feed at half the recommended rate. As larger or stronger-growing bulbs increase in size it may be beneficial to pot on; but do not overpot. When bulbs reach flowering size, the same kinds can be removed from their individual pots and put together in a pan.

Rather than pot each bulblet separately in the autumn/fall following germination, it may be preferable to plant out the pot of seedlings into a compartment on a bulb bed. Instead of even-sowing seed in pots, it is better to sow directly into a compartment of the bulb bed. Remove an inch (25 mm) of soil and replace it with a soil-based seed compost, level, firm and space-sow or sow thinly, barely cover and then label.

Vegetative Propagation

As well as being storage organs, bulbs can also be organs of regeneration that can be manipulated by a propagator. Horticulturally, bulbs include true bulbs, corms, tubers, rhizomes and pseudobulbs. True bulbs are of two types: tunicated with an outer protective dry scale, as in an onion, or non-tunicated where the outer overlapping scales are fleshy, for example *Fritillaria*.

Tunicated Bulbs
A few tunicated bulbs are of annual duration, such as tulips and the reticulata group of *Iris*. During the production of aerial growth, the original bulb disintegrates to be replaced by a cluster of new bulbs of varying sizes. In a fertile soil during a wet spring there will be more and larger bulbs than in a starved soil during a dry spring. When the foliage in this group has died down, the new bulb clusters should be sorted through and graded. Use the largest bulbs for flowering in the following season whilst the smaller ones will need to be grown on. Tulips increase at an acceptable rate. In the reticulata group of

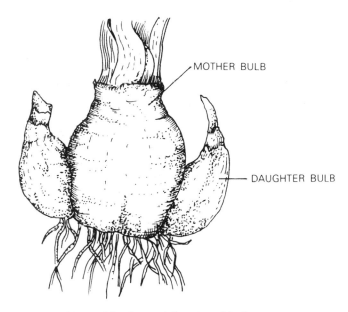

Figure 33   Perennial tunicated bulb

Iris there is a steady increase in new bulbs but few of them will be of flowering size. Deep planting (6in/150mm or more) will induce more regular flowering, but bulb increase can be slow.

Most tunicated bulbs are perennial, budding off daughter bulbs which remain attached to the mother and continue to increase in size. Periodically bulbs should be lifted when dormant and the daughter bulbs detached (*see* Fig. 34).

The larger of these will be of flowering size but the smaller ones will need to be grown on. The increase of most bulbs is at an acceptable rate; with some it can be so rapid that the bulbs become invasive (for example *Muscari armenia-cum*) whilst at the other extreme it can be very slow (for example garden hyacinths). As the increase of garden hyacinths is too slow for commercial purposes, artificial means were devised to increase this rate, often referred to as 'cuttage'. Garden hyacinths are not bulbs for the rock garden, although the wild species from which they have been developed, *Hyacinthus orientalis*, would be acceptable. Other bulbs that will respond to this treatment are species of *Pancratium, Vallota, Cyrtanthus, Sprekelia, Lycoris* and *Hippeastrum*. This treatment is carried out when bulbs are dormant, usually in summer. Bulbs are lifted or removed from their pots, loose scales rubbed off and if there are perennial roots, these are removed. There are three types of cuttage: scoring, scooping and coring.

SCORING: three cuts are made across the diameter of the bulb plate deep enough to destroy the growth/flower bud.

SCOOPING: the entire bulb plate is removed with a low pyramid consisting of the base of the bulb scales taking out the flower/growth bud.

CORING: using a cork borer or a potato parer, a cylinder of tissue is taken out in the centre of the basal plate about 1in (25mm) in depth, which will remove the flower/growth bud.

All cut surfaces should be dusted with flowers of sulphur or a fungicide such as Captan, Benlate or Thiram. Stand the bulbs base upwards in boxes/flats of dry sand in a warm, dry and light place until the cut surfaces have callused. Put the bulbs into polythene bags with moist peat, bark fibre or sphagnum moss; tie the bag, label and store in a warm, dry, dark place such as an airing cupboard for three months. During this time bulblets will form within the treated bulbs.

By the time treatment is complete it will be autumn/fall and lower soil temperatures will mean that bulbs can be planted out into a nursery bed. With one or just a few bulbs it will be better to pot each separately or to use a deep box, tray or flat and a soil-based compost. These containers should be put into a frame or under other form of protection without heat and with the compost kept no more than just moist until new root growth begins when watering can be increased. Continue regular watering until growth begins to yellow when the compost is dried off. When lifted it will be found that a cluster of small bulbs has replaced the original. These are separated, graded and replanted or repotted in

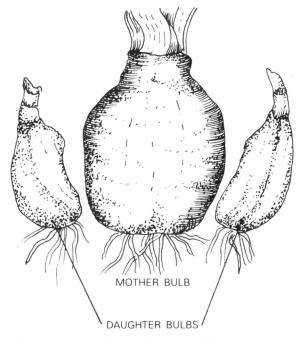

MOTHER BULB

DAUGHTER BULBS

Figure 34   Daughter bulbs detached from mother

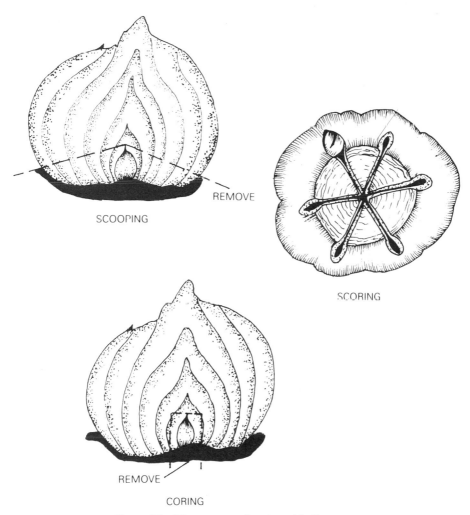

SCOOPING

REMOVE

SCORING

REMOVE

CORING

Figure 35   Three types of tunicated bulb cuttage

autumn/fall and grown on until they reach flowering size. The length of time this will take depends on the species and subsequent treatment. Coring takes the shortest time—two to three years—but will produce the fewest bulbs; scooping will be longest (four to six years) but there will be most new bulbs, whilst scoring is intermediate in time and number.

Twin scaling is a modification of this method which has become extensively used for the commercial production of *Narcissus*. It is quite suitable for all the genera mentioned for cuttage and has been successful with species of *Galanthus, Leucojum, Muscari, Ornithogalum, Placea, Scilla, Chionodoxa, Chionoscilla* and *Sterbergia*. It is possible that this technique can be used for all

63

perennial bulbs, but those of annual duration do not seem to respond to this treatment.

Lift the bulbs as soon as the foliage dies down, discarding any that are damaged or not totally healthy; remove all extraneous matter—old leaves and flower stems, roots, loose scales and soil. Cleanliness is important at all stages, so ensure there is a clean working surface and cutting implements have been sterilised in a flame or by dipping into surgical spirit; before treatment the cleaned bulbs should be steeped for one minute in surgical spirit or one per cent formalin solution.

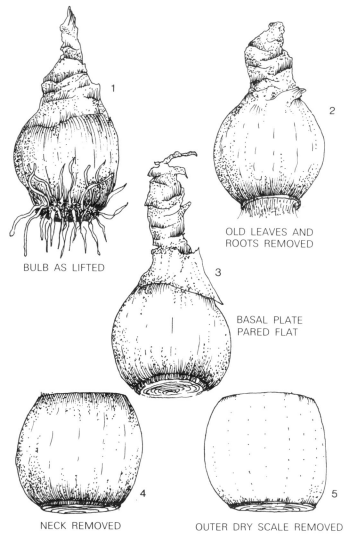

Figure 36   Twin scaling (A)

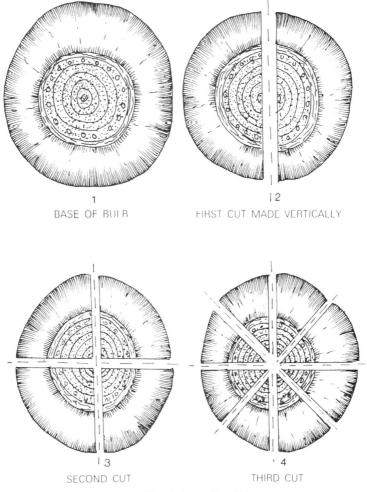

1
BASE OF BULB

|2
FIRST CUT MADE VERTICALLY

|3
SECOND CUT

'4
THIRD CUT

Figure 37   Twin scaling (B)

Cut the bulb vertically into two equal pieces across the diameter of the basal plate and then cut each half into quarters through the basal place. Using a knife, the largest bulbs can be cut into eight pieces. A scalpel will be better for smaller bulbs, which should be cut into four pieces. Using a scalpel or razor blade, make a transverse cut through the basal plate so that each piece has two scales; discard the central portion of the bulb at the apex of the slice which will contain the remnants of growing/flowering bud. Dust the pieces with powdered Thiram, Benlate or Captan so that each is coated with a film of fungicide. Pack treated scales into polythene bags, using twice the volume of moist sand. Seal each bag with a twist of wire or elastic band, allowing plenty of air to be trapped within, and attach a label. Store the bags in the dark for twelve weeks at a temperature of between 60° and 70°F (15–21°C); an airing cupboard is quite

65

suitable. The period of twelve weeks should be used as a guide, as species will respond differently. Inspect after eight weeks and then at weekly intervals until a bulblet can be discerned between the scales. On removal from the polythene bag, the scales can be lined out in trays/flats so that their tips just protrude from a well-drained soil-based compost. By now autumn/fall will be well advanced and containers should be kept under protection but without heat: keep the compost just moist. Shoot growth may begin immediately but it is more likely to be delayed until spring. As root and shoot growth develop, increase water and continue until the shoots begin to yellow, when it should be reduced. The time taken for bulbs to reach flowering size following twin scaling will vary from two to five years, depending on kind and subsequent cultivation following lining out.

Non-tunicated Bulbs

These are found only in the genera *Lilium*, *Fritillaria* and *Nomocharis*. The best-known non-tunicated bulbs are species of *Lilium*. Only a few of these are small enough for a rock or peat garden.

The more common are species *L. formosanum* var. *pricei*, *L. pomponium* and *L. tenuifolium* (*pumilum*); there are a few others but these are rare. Whenever possible lilies should be raised from seed for health reasons; all three mentioned are easy and can be in flower within two years. When seed is not available, or there is an especially good form, vegetative propagation can be tried. Bulbs should be lifted following flowering, as they are easier to find with the old flower stem still attached. Whilst out of the ground their bulbs and

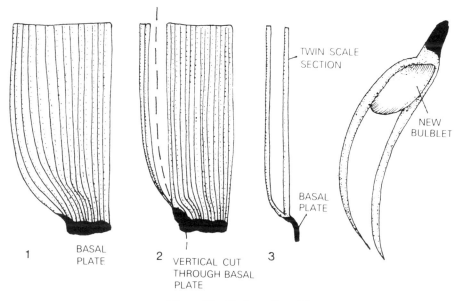

Figure 38   Twin scaling (C)

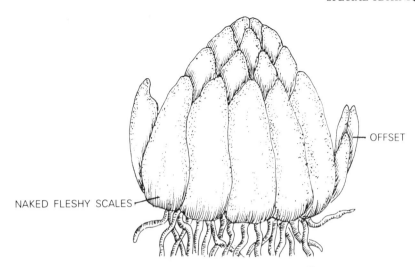

OFFSET

NAKED FLESHY SCALES

Figure 39 Non-tunicated bulb with offset

basal roots hould be protected from drying out by storing in moist peat, bark fibre or sand. These lilies will increase by budding off secondary bulbs which can be separated. It may be that there will be bulblets around the base of the mother bulb or on the portion of stem between bulb and soil level. These bulblets are detached and can be lined out in a nursery bed or a box/flat, pot or pan using a well-drained organic soil (*see* Fig. 40).

All lilies can be increased from scales. At lifting take off a few of the outer scales, although some will have become detached naturally. Half of each scale should be pushed into a mixture of equal parts of moist peat and sand in trays/ flats or pans; it is better if the exposed parts of the scales are covered with moist sphagnum moss. An alternative is to pack the scales in a polythene bag with twice the volume of moist sphagnum moss. Keep the containers in a cool shaded place where they are just moist for a period of eight to twelve weeks. Periodic inspections will eventually show the development of a bulblet at the base of the scale. At this stage the scale should be transplanted into a lime-free, well drained peaty soil with the scale tip just protruding. Keep under protection but without heat, ensuring the compost does not become excessively wet. When aerial growth begins to yellow at the end of summer, reduce the amount of water. They may then be removed from their containers and planted out in a nursery bed or singly in pots (*see* Fig. 41).

The next biggest group of non-tunicated bulbs, is the fritillaria. Only a few have bulbs as large as lillies, but all kinds can be increased by scales. Mostly the bulbs are small and often consist of only two scales; these can be divided and potted separately. In others there can be a mass-production of pin-head sized bulblets collectively known as rice. Gather together all this rice and sow like large seeds on the surface of a well-drained organic soil and just cover. Keep

67

under protection but without heat. These need handling each year and it is best at this time to grade them.

Natural increase of bulbs of *Nomocharis* is always slow although they too can be increased by using scales. As the bulbs are not large, detach only one or two scales at any one time.

Corms

When there are favourable conditions a corm will start into growth. Two kinds of roots will be produced from the base: the usual feeding ones and thicker

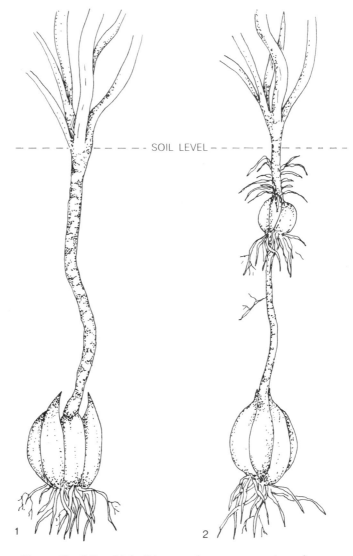

Figure 40   Lily with bulblet on subterranean portion of stem

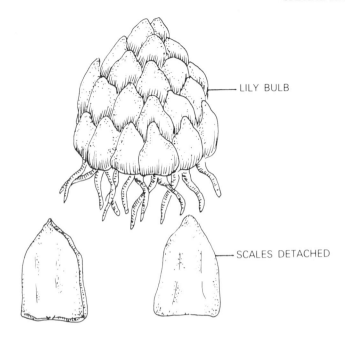

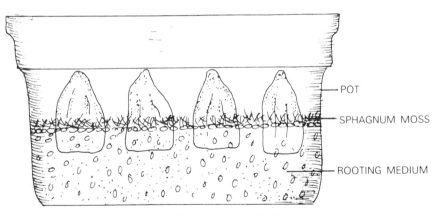

Figure 41   Propagation of lily by scales

contractile roots which pull the corm down into the soil to a desired level. While there is aerial growth, a new corm is developing on top of the old which is shrivelling and becoming compressed as stored food is being used. If lifted after the aerial parts have died away, it will be seen that on top of the remnants of the old is one or a few new large corms of flowering size. Around the corm there may be a number of tiny cormlets attached by threads known collectively as spawn. This spawn is collected and stored in moist peat, bark fibre or sand over winter. In spring, it is soaked for 24 hours in cold water and then sown on the surface of a soil-based compost and just covered; it is better kept under protection but without heat. When the aerial parts have again died away corms of varying size will be found; grade them and grow on the smallest. New corm production can be increased by cutting out the terminal growth-bud just prior to planting. Flowering is unlikely, but axillary buds that have been forced into growth will produce a cluster of shoots and at the base of each will be found a

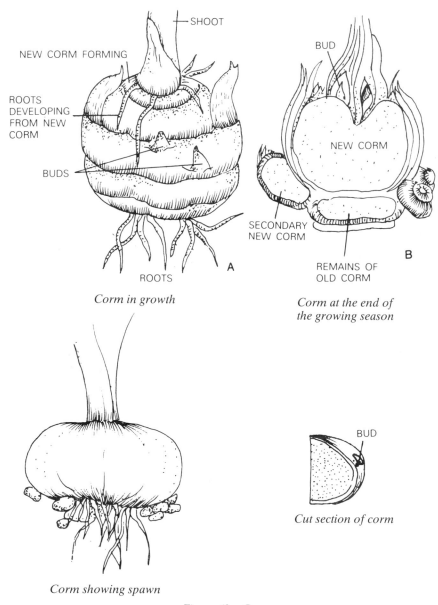

SHOOT

NEW CORM FORMING

BUD

ROOTS DEVELOPING FROM NEW CORM

NEW CORM

BUDS

SECONDARY NEW CORM

ROOTS

A

REMAINS OF OLD CORM

B

Corm in growth

Corm at the end of the growing season

BUD

Cut section of corm

Corm showing spawn

Figure 42   Corms

70

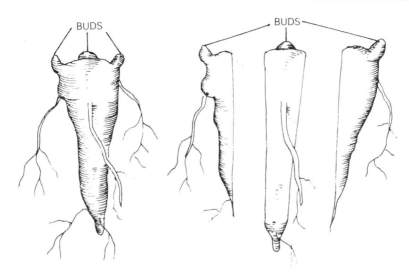

Figure 43   Root tuber cut into pieces

new corm. The larger corms, such as *Gladiolus blandus*, can be increased by cutting. Strip off the tunic prior to planting, remove the terminal growth bud and cut the corm into pieces ensuring that there is one bud on each piece. Dust the pieces with a fungicide before planting either in a nursery bed or in trays/flats, pots or pans in a soil-based compost. When the aerial growth has died away, each piece will be found to have produced a new corm.

Tubers
Natural increase by stem tubers can be slow, but the propagator can speed this up by cutting. Using a sharp knife cut into pieces, each with a bud, prior to planting in beds, trays/flats, pots or pans. All cut surfaces should be dusted with fungicide.

Those plants that have tubers in the form of swollen roots can be divided prior to planting. With well-developed roots ensure that there is a portion of stem with buds. The other type, which has a compressed tap root, should be cut into pieces ensuring there is at least one bud on each; dust all cut surfaces with a fungicide. Division of all tubers is better delayed until buds are swelling, when their position is more easily seen and it is obvious where to make the cuts.

Rhizomes
Rhizomes should be lifted immediately following flowering, when all side branches with terminal growing points can be detached. Dust cut surfaces with a fungicide and replant to the same depth in the rock garden or pot each piece separately. If portions of rhizome without growing points are boxed with their upper parts exposed, many will produce new growing points if kept under protection (*see* Fig. 44).

71

Pseudobulbs

Pseudobulbs are best divided just prior to the commencement of new growth. Species and cultivars of *Pleione* are probably the most popular terrestrial orchids with pseudobulbs. As with most epiphytes, these grow better when they are crowded together in a compost made of predominantly fibrous peat or a medium-grade bark fibre. These are best handled just before flower buds begin to swell, in early spring or even in late winter; at this stage there will be no roots, or at the most just rudimentary roots which must not be damaged. Start watering as the flowers fade and continue until the new foliage begins to turn yellow in autumn/fall. Once growth is well developed, apply a weak liquid feed at two-weekly intervals. This will provide a quantity of large plump pseudo-bulbs at the end of the season.

Often there may be clusters of tiny pseudobulbs produced on the tips of mature new ones. Collect these together and put as many into a small pot as can be accommodated—the more the better. Start careful watering in early spring, making sure that the compost does not become overwet, and continue until the growth yellows. No watering is necessary when the leaves have died away, although the compost should never be allowed to become dust dry.

Ferns

Spores produced by ferns are different organisms from seed, because they have not resulted from the fertilisation of an ovule. In ferns there are two plant forms—known as sporophyte and gametophyte. The sporophyte, which has the leafy frond and is readily recognisable as a fern, produces spores which,

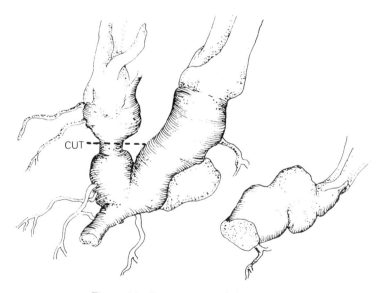

Figure 44   Propagation of rhizomatous iris

given suitable conditions, germinate and develop into the gametophyte. This is a minute organism known as a prothallus which will produce male and female cells.

In most ferns, the fronds produce sori on the undersurface of the pinnae, which when ripe dehisce to liberate spores. There is, however, a group of ferns in which there are two different kinds of fronds: one that is the same as other ferns but has no sori, whilst the other has become specialised in spore production only—for example *Blechnum* species.

Collect spore-bearing fronds when the sori are fully developed but before the spore cases have ruptured. Wrap the fronds carefully in sheets of news-paper, then put the packages into paper bags, seal them and keep them in a warm, dry place. As the fronds dry, moisture is absorbed by the newspaper which also retains the released spores. Spores are dust-like and extremely light so that if disturbed they float into the air and remain in suspension for long periods. In a warm dry autumn/fall the air can be filled with many kinds of floating spores.

To raise ferns absolute hygiene is necessary to protect them from infection and against invasion by alien spores. Pans or shallow pots of either clay or plastic should be sterilised in boiling water or a formalin solution. When the pots are dry and there is no longer any smell of formalin put them into clean polythene bags until ready for use. Use a compost of equal parts of soil, sand and peat with each ingredient sterilised. Put 1–2in (25–50mm) of the compost into pots or pans, firm and level off the surface. Sow the spores in an enclosed area where the air is still; when a number of kinds of ferns are to be sown, try to do them on different days to reduce alien spores invading the containers. Spread the spores as thinly as possible on the surface of moist compost and cover the container immediately with a sheet of glass which has previously been sterilised. Stand the pots or pans permanently in saucers of water and keep them in a warm shady place. Spores should always be sown as soon as possible after collecting. Germination can take from two weeks to more than a year.

Another method, which reduces disturbance of spores, is to take a frond or a portion of frond just prior to the sori rupturing and place it on the surface of the compost in a pan or pot which is covered with glass and stood in a saucer of water. As the spore cases rupture the spores will fall onto the surface of the compost.

Looking through the glass, it will be noticed that the surface of the compost is becoming green with a moss-like growth which will eventually become liverwort-like. Under a lens it will be seen that there are tiny leaf-like structures that are heart- or kidney-shaped and which can reach $\frac{1}{2}$in (12mm) across. These are the prothalli. When the prothalli are mature the male cells in the film of water surrounding the prothallus will swim towards the archegonia where they will fuse with the female cells. Following fertilisation a spore-bearing plant will develop and will eventually become recognisable with miniature fronds. If there are controlled temperatures and humidity the sporelings can be potted singly or in patches into the same compost in the smallest possible pots.

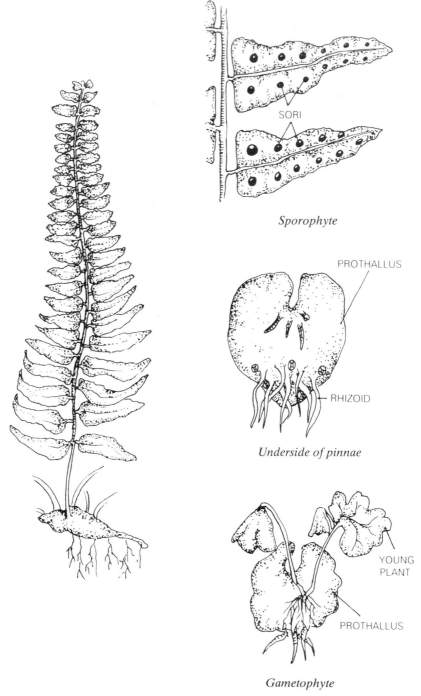

Sporophyte

Underside of pinnae

Gametophyte

Figure 45   Parts of a fern

It is more usual for the sporelings to be allowed to develop into recognisable plants before potting. At all times the potted sporelings should be kept in shady enclosed conditions with a high humidity. Rather than water from the top, pots should be stood permanently in saucers on trays of water. When plants are growing strongly this high humidity should gradually be reduced until eventually the pots can be stood on an open bench or in a closed frame out-of-doors. Here watering can be from above.

Mature ferns can be increased vegetatively. Most produce multiple crowns and these can be separated along with some roots when dormant; the best time is just prior to recommencement of growth. In the walking fern, *Camptosorus rhizophilus*, if the tip of a frond touches the ground a new plant will grow. *Asplenium bulbiferum* is well known for the embryo plants that appear on the edges of pinnae. If these are carefully detached and pricked out into the type of compost already mentioned, new plants will develop from each. An alternative is to detach a newly developed frond and lay it on the surface of a box/flat full of compost. Insert a section of petiole into the compost and bring the pinnae into touch with the compost with small stones. Cover the box/flat with a sheet of glass and keep in a warm and shady place until the leaf embryos have developed into plants. This treatment can be successful in inducing plantlets to form with some other species and/or forms of *Asplenium*, and *Nephrolepis*.

Some ferns have rhizomes, for example *Davillia, Phymatodes* and *Pyrrosia*. These tend to be epiphytic in nature, growing over or up rocks or tree trunks. When containerised the rhizomes soon grow out of the pots in which they are being grown. These rhizomes can be detached whilst dormant and pinned down on the surface of the compost in a container where they will eventually produce roots and a new plant.

Part Two

Recommended Propagation Methods for Individual Plants

Introduction to the A–Z

My definition of an alpine plant is any plant small enough to be grown in a medium rock garden, irrespective of the altitude from whence it originated. As already mentioned, this book is intended for use by gardeners of temperate regions of either hemisphere. Climates of countries in these regions will have variable winter minimum temperatures so there are genera that may be tender in colder countries. The inclusion of certain plants may surprise some gardeners, but what is a weed in one country can be highly desirable in another and vice versa. Grasses have been omitted, so have cacti and succulents, even those that are botanical alpines, as these have their own specialised societies. A genus has been included if there is even one species small enough for a rock garden or if there are dwarf cultivars of a normally large species. When a species immediately follows a genus it means that it is monotypic or there is one species only that is suited to a rock garden. Every attempt has been made to be up to date in nomenclature but names that have had long usage have been retained. There is cross reference for alternative generic names or where species may have been reclassified. Family names and genera follow Willis (1973) in the main, except where there have been recent revisions, such as the old Liliaceae, which has been split into many new families.

The letter H and numbers that appear at the end of entries indicate hardiness, and are based on hardiness zones used in the USA. There are ten zones but I have used only the top five, which I consider applicable to temperate regions. Temperatures that appear in the list below are winter minimums:

zone   6: $-10°$ to $0°$F $(-29°$ to $-23°$C)
zone   7: $0°$ to $10°$F $(-23°$ to $-17°)$
zone   8: $10°$ to $20°$F $(-12°$ to -7C)
zone   9: $20°$ to $30°$F $(-7°$ to $-1°$C)
zone 10: $30°$ to $40°$F $(-1°$ to $5°$C)

Hardiness is difficult to determine, since so many factors affect it. With plant habitat there is latitude, altitude, distance from the sea and prevailing winds. As well as the place of origin, conditions of cultivation within the garden have to be considered: in summer, the amount of sunshine, temperatures and their duration; in winter the times of the first and last frosts, winter extremes and their duration, frost penetration and wind exposure. There is also annual rainfall and the season at which most falls to be considered: does it fall as snow in winter and is there permanent cover? Is winter cold and dry, or is cold combined with wetness when there is no snow cover? Of equal importance is the condition of growth; is it active or dormant, hard or succulent? Hardiness can vary within the same part of the country—for example a town can be warmer than nearby country areas; hardiness of the same plant can even vary when planted in different positions within the same garden. The hardiness zones that are given are my determinations and are intended only as a guide. Often more than one figure appears, which means that the plant does not fit cleanly into either. With large genera that have wide distribution, it is inevitable that there are going to be some plants much hardier than others.

Mode of growth of species within a genus is given with a few words on occasions to indicate quality. Method of propagation can be assumed to refer to all species unless exceptions are recorded. Where a number of different methods are given, the reader must choose the one which is best suited to his or her requirements. There are genera that contain newly introduced or reintroduced species from the wild. When more experience in cultivation is gained, better methods of propagation may be discovered.

A–Z Listing of Plants

Abies (Pinaceae)
Forest trees of which a few species have produced cultivars small enough for a larger rock garden. Stem cuttings of current season's growth taken in winter can sometimes be induced to root. Cleft or side grafting onto seedlings of the same species is an alternative. H6–8

Abeliophyllum distichum (Oleaceae)
Low sprawling deciduous shrub. Sow seed in spring. Take stem cuttings in late summer. Its natural habit often results in the lowest branches coming down to soil level and rooting. Pinning down stems will aid rooting. H7

Abromeitiella (Bromeliaceae)
Rosette-forming perennial making low mounds. Sow seed in spring. Separate individual rosettes when not in active growth. If without roots treat as cuttings. H9

Abronia (Nyctaginaceae)
Annuals or perennials of varying sizes. Sow seed in spring. Take stem cuttings of new growth in spring. H9

Abrotanella forsterioides (Compositae)
Cushion-forming sub-shrub. Sow fertile seed in spring, but because of short viability it is better to sow immediately it has been collected. Take off individual rosettes of new mature growth carefully from the perimeter of the cushion so as not to spoil symmetry and treat as cuttings. H8

Acaena (Rosaceae)
Low-growing or prostrate perennials, forming carpets whose stems can become woody with age. In favourable conditions some species can be invasive. Although cold stimulates germination, seed can be spring sown. Take stem cuttings in late summer or lift at the end of winter and pull apart. H8–9

Acantholimon (Plumbaginaceae)
Rosette-forming perennials that can form mounds. Sow seed in spring. Late summer cuttings root erratically. H8

Acanthophyllum (Caryophyllaceae)
Perennials, often cushion-like and spiny, stems becoming woody with age. Sow seed in spring. Late summer stem cuttings root erratically. H8

Acarpha (Calyceraceae)
Perennials, not easy to cultivate. Sow fertile seed in spring. Divide established clumps as they come into growth. Success variable. H8

Aceras anthropophorum (Orchidaceae)
Terrestrial orchid. Divide immediately after flowering. H8

Acerophyllum rossii (Saxifragaceae)
Perennial. Sow seed in spring. Divide following flowering. H8

Achillea (Compositae)
Perennials of varying size, habits and quality. Sow seed in spring. Divide clumps in spring as growth starts. Take stem cuttings of mature new growth in autumn/fall. H6–8

Achlys (Podophyllaceae)
Perennial. Seed can be sown in spring, although cold stimulates germination. Divide established clumps as they start into growth. H8

Acinos see *Calamintha*

Aciphylla (Umbelliferae)
Dioecious perennials the stems of which can become woody with age. Variable in size. Spiny leaves may form only a single rosette which can be monocarpic. In some species rosettes may form a dome or carpet. Seedlings resulting from spring-sown fertile seed are soft and carrot-like, very different from the leathery leaves of the adult form. Rosettes taken off the mat-forming species and treated as cuttings in late summer will root. H7–8

Aconitum (Ranunculaceae)
Perennials of varying sizes, a few only being suited to a rock garden. Sow seed in autumn/fall and expose to winter cold; germination can be erratic and delayed. Divide as plants start into growth. H6–8

Acorus gramineus (Araceae)
Perennial whose forms are more desirable than the species. Divide as plants start into growth. H8

Actinea see *Hymenoxys*

Actinella see *Hymenoxys*

Actinotus (Umbelliferae)
Perennials, often short lived and treated as annuals. Size and quality variable. Sow seed in spring. H10

Adenandra (Rutaceae)
Evergreen shrubs of variable sizes and habits. Sow seed in spring. Take stem cuttings of new mature growth in autumn/fall. H9–10

Adenophora (Campanulaceae)
Perennials of varying sizes. Sow seed in spring. Divide established clumps as they start into growth. H7–8

Adesmia (Leguminosae)
Evergreen shrubs of varying sizes. Spring sow seed after soaking for 24 hours in water. Take stem cuttings in late summer of non-flowering new growth. H7–8

Adiantum (Adiantaceae)
Maidenhair ferns of varying sizes. Divide as plants start into growth. H7–10

Adlumia fungosa (Fumariaceae)
Weak climber for draping over shrubs; short lived perennial. Sow seed in spring. H8

Adonis (Ranunculaceae)
Annuals and perennials. Sow seed as soon as collected for best germination; old seed germinates erratically even when exposed to cold and can be delayed. Some of the so-called doubles produce seed and this seems to breed true. Divide following flowering. H7

Adoxa moschatellina (Adoxaceae)
Summer-dormant rhizomatous perennial, more curious than beautiful. Sow seed immediately it is ripe. Divide or separate following flowering. H7

Aeonium (Crassulaceae)
Rosette-forming succulents, most of which are too big for a rock garden. Sow seed in spring. Take off new rosettes in late summer and if without roots, treat as cuttings. H9–10

Aethionema (Cruciferae)
Annuals and low-growing perennials of varying qualities. Sow seed in spring. Take stem cuttings of new non-flowering growth in summer. H8–9

Aichryson (Crassulaceae)
Biennial or short-lived perennials. Sow seed in spring. Take stem cuttings of perennials in early spring. H10

Ajuga (Labiatae)
Annuals and perennials. Sow seed in spring. Established plants can be lifted and pulled apart when new growth is complete. H6–7

Albuca (Hyacinthaceae)
Winter-dormant bulbs of varying sizes. Sow seed in spring. Separate bulbs when dormant; twin scaling. H10

Alchemilla (Rosaceae)
Perennials or sub-shrubs. Northern hemisphere species are better autumn/fall sown and exposed to winter cold whereas those from the southern hemisphere can be spring sown. Divide as plants start into growth. The shrubby species can be increased by taking stem cuttings of non-flowering growth in autumn/fall. H6–9

Alkanna (Boraginaceae)
Biennials and perennials, often short lived. Sow seed in spring. Divide as plants start into growth. Take root cuttings in autumn/fall. H8–9

Allardia see *Waldheimia*

Allium (Alliaceae)
A large genus of aromatic perennials with underground storage organs, mostly bulbs, a few are rhizomes. Plants are of variable sizes and quality and some can be weeds. In a few species, e.g. *A. roseum*, bulbils may form in the inflorescence but these should not be used for propagation. Sow seed in spring. Separate bulbs when dormant; divide rhizomes when not in active growth. H6–9

Alonsoa (Scrophulariaceae)
Perennials. Sow seed in spring. Take stem cuttings in spring. H8–9

Aloysia see *Lippia*

Alstroemeria (Alstroemeriaceae)
Rhizomatous perennials. Some species can be invasive, sizes variable. Seed has short viability and is best sown immediately it is ripe. Division following flowering, although successful, can be variable. H8

Alternanthera (Amaranthaceae)
Small perennials the cultivars of which have handsome foliage. Divide in spring or at this season take stem cuttings. H10

Alyssum (Cruciferae)
(Species sometimes included in this genus may also be found in *Aurina*, *Lobularia* and *Ptilotrichum*.) Annuals and low-growing perennials. Sow seed in spring. Established clumps can be lifted in summer following completion of new growth and pulled apart. Take stem cuttings from the new growth following flowering in summer. H8

Amana see *Tulipa*

Amaracus see *Origanum*

Amorpha (Leguminosae)
Deciduous and evergreen shrubs of varying sizes, mostly too big for a rock garden. Soak seed for 24 hours in cold water before spring sowing. Take stem cuttings of non-flowering growth when possible in late summer. H8–9

Amphoricarpus (Compositae)
Perennials. Sow seed in spring. Divide as growth is about to start. H8

Amsonia (Apocynaceae)
Perennials of varying sizes. Sow seed in spring. Divide as new growth starts. H8

Anacamptis pyramidalis (Orchidaceae)
Terrestrial orchid. Divide following flowering. H8

Anacyclus (Compositae)
Perennials that can be short lived. Sow seed in spring. Take stem cuttings of non-flowering growth if possible, in late summer. H8

Anagallis (Primulaceae)
Annuals and perennials that can be short lived. Sow seed in spring. Take stem cuttings in summer of non-flowering growth. H8–9

Anaphalis (Compositae)
Perennials of varying sizes. Sow seed in spring. Take stem cuttings in autumn/fall. Divide as plants start into growth. H7

Anchusa (Boraginaceae)
Perennials of varying sizes and qualities. Seed is sown in spring; divide following flowering. *A. caespitosa* is a desirable species of which young plants flower best so propagation should take place every second year. Take root cuttings of this and other species in summer. H7–8

Ancylostemon (Gesneriaceae)
Rosette-forming perennials. Sow seed in spring on chopped sphagnum moss. Divide established clumps as they start into growth. Prepare leaf cuttings from mature new leaves. H9

Androcymbium (Colchicaceae)
Corms. Sow seed in spring. Separate corms when not in active growth. H8–9

Andromeda polifolia (Ericaceae)
Evergreen shrub of variable habit. Sow seed in spring on chopped sphagnum moss. Take stem cuttings of new growth in late summer. Layer low shoots in early autumn/fall. H7

Androsace (Primulaceae)
Perennials of variable habit: cushions, clumps and plants with runners. Seed which can be spring sown is better handled immediately following collection. Clump formers can be divided after flowering or when new growth is complete. Individual rosettes of new mature growth can be taken carefully from perimeter so as not so spoil the cushion and treated as cuttings. Stoloniferous species, e.g. *A. stolonifera*, behave like strawberries. If plantlets do not root naturally, put a stone on the stolon near the new plant. H7–8

Andryala (Compositae)
Perennials, often short lived. Sow seed in spring. H8

Anemone (Ranunculaceae)
(This genus has contained species now classified with *Pulsatilla*.) A large genus of perennials of differing sizes and qualities; some have tubers. Seed can be sown in spring, but fresh seed germinates better than old, which can be erratic and long delayed; cold sometimes improves germination. Non-tuberous species can be divided as they start into growth. Tubers are cut into pieces whilst dormant. H6–9

Anemonella thalictroides (Ranunculaceae)
Tuberous perennial. Sow fresh seed, which germinates best. With old seed winter cold will speed up and improve germination. Double flower forms, which are most desired, are lifted when dormant and separated. H8

Anemopsis californica (Saururaceae)
Running prostrate, rather coarse, moisture-loving perennial which in favourable positions can be invasive. Sow seed as fresh as possible. Plants root at the nodes as they grow so that new plants can be detached at almost any time. H10

Anguillaria see **Wurmbea**

Anisotome (Umbelliferae)
Dioecious aromatic foliage plants. Sow fertile seed in spring. Most species have a single tap root but in some there can be side rosettes attached to it; these are detached after new growth is complete and if without fibrous roots treated as cuttings. H8

Anomatheca (Iridaceae)
(Species within this genus have been and may still be found in *Lapeirousia*.) Winter-dormant corms, but often treated as annuals. Sow seed in spring. Separate corms when dormant. H8–9

Antennaria (Compositae)
Mat-forming perennials. Sow fertile seed in spring. Detach individual rosettes after completion of new growth and treat as cuttings. Lift established plants following flowering and pull apart. H7

Anthemis (Compositae)
Perennials varying sizes and qualities. Sow seed in spring. Divide established clumps as they start into growth. Take stem cuttings of new non-flowering growth in late summer. H7–8

Anthericum (Anthericaceae)
Rhizomatous perennials. Sow seed in spring; germination can sometimes be delayed. Divide established clumps as new growth starts. H8

Anthyllis (Leguminosae)
Perennials and shrubs. Sow seed in spring after soaking in cold water for 24 hours. Take cuttings of new non-flowering growth in late summer. H8

Antirrhinum (Scrophulariaceae)
(Asarina may be included with Antirrhinum.) Perennials, although some species which are short lived may be treated as annuals. Sow seed in spring. Take stem cuttings of non-flowering growth in summer. H9

Aotus (Leguminosae)
Evergreen shrubs of varying sizes. Sow seed in spring after soaking in boiling water for 24 hours. Stem cuttings of mature growth are taken in late summer. H10

Aphyllanthes monspeliensis (Aphyllanthaccae)
Perennial. Sow seed in spring. Divide following flowering. H9

Aplopappus see *Haplopappus*

Aquilegia (Ranunculaceae)
Perennials of varying sizes. Most species are promiscuous and seed should be collected only from plants grown in isolation. Fresh seed germinates best. Spring sowing is satisfactory for most species, but winter cold stimulates germination especially with old seed. Division can be practised with stronger-growing species following flowering. H7–8

Arabis (Cruciferae)
Annuals and perennials of variable quality, some are weedy. Sow seed in spring. Divide after flowering or take stem cuttings of new mature growth. H7–9

Archeria (Epacridaceae)
Small evergreen shrubs. Sow seed on chopped sphagnum moss in spring; germination is difficult and erratic. Take stem cuttings of new growth in late summer; success is variable. H9

Arcterica nana (Ericaceae)
Evergreen shrub. Sow seed in spring on chopped sphagnum moss. Take stem cuttings of new growth in late summer. H7

Arctomecon (Papaveraceae)
Short-lived perennials which are not easy. Sow seed in spring. H9

Arctostaphylos (Ericaceae)
Evergreen shrubs of varying sizes and habits. Sow seed on chopped sphagnum moss in spring; germination can be erratic and difficult. Take stem cuttings of new growth in late summer; success variable. Prostrate and low-growing species can be layered in autumn/fall. H7–9

Arctotis see *Osteospermum*

Arctous alpina (Ericaceae)
Prostrate deciduous sub-shrub. Sow seed after extraction from berries and sow in spring on chopped sphagnum moss. Take soft stem cuttings of new spring growth. H6

Arenaria (Caryophyllaceae)
Perennials in which one or two species can become woody with age. Variable in habit and quality. Sow seed in spring. Carpeting species often root as they grow. Divide as they start into growth. Take cuttings of non-flowering growth in summer. H8

Ardisia (Myrsinaceae)
Evergreen shrubs and trees of which a few are small enough for a rock garden. Sow seed after extracting from fruit in spring. Take stem cuttings of new non-flowering growth in autumn/fall. H9–10

Aretiastrum (Valerianaceae)
Perennials, which can become woody with age, form mats, cushions or domes. Sow seed in spring. Take stem cuttings in late summer. H8

Argemone (Papaveraceae)
Annuals or short-lived perennials. Sow seed in spring. H8–9

Arisaema (Araceae)
Tuberous perennials of varying sizes; peduncle can continue to elongate after flowering. Sow seed as soon as possible after extracting from fruit, although spring is more usual. Cut tubers into pieces whilst dormant. H9–10

Arisarum (Araceae)
Tuberous perennials. Sow seed as fresh as possible for best germination. Divide established clumps after flowering. H8

Aristea (Iridaccac)
Rhizomatous perennials of varying sizes. Sow seed in spring. Divide as plants start into growth, ensuring that there are roots on each fan. H9–10

Aristolochia (Aristolochiaceae)
Perennials and woody climbers of which a few are small enough for a rock garden. Sow seed in spring. Divide established clumps as plants start into growth. Take cuttings of non-flowering growth in late summer. H8–10

Armeria (Plumbaginaceae)
Perennials forming mounds or tufts. Sow seed in spring. Clumps can be lifted and pulled apart before they start into growth. Individual tufts can be detached and treated as cuttings in late summer. H8–9

Arnebia (Boraginaceae)
Perennials. Sow seed in spring. Divide as plants go out of flower. H9

Arnica (Compositae)
Perennials often short lived. Sow fertile seed in spring. Divide as they finish flowering. H6

Artemisia (Compositae)
Annuals, perennials and shrubs of varying sizes, habits and qualities. Sow fertile seed in spring. Divide clump formers as they start into growth. Take stem cuttings of new non-flowering growth in autumn/fall. *A. absinthum* 'Lambrooks Silver' roots best when stem cuttings are taken in early summer. H6–9

Arthropodium cirrhatum (Anthericaceae)
Perennial. Sow seed in spring. Divide established clumps as they start into growth. H9

Arum (Araceae)
Tuberous perennials of varying sizes and quality. Sow seed in spring. Separate or divide tubers when dormant. H8–9

Asarina (Scrophulariaceae)
(Some species may still be found with *Antirrhinum.*) Perennial sprawlers. Sow seed in spring. Take stem cuttings, if possible of non-flowering growth, in autumn/fall. H8

89

Asarum (Aristolochiaceae)
Tuberous perennials the leaves of which are more attractive than the bizarre flowers. Sow seed as fresh as possible. Divide when not in active growth. H8–10

Asperula (Rubiaceae)
Perennials. Sow seed in spring. Take stem cuttings of new growth produced after flowering. H8

Asphodelus acaulis (Asphodelaceae)
Tuberous perennial. Sow seed in spring. H9

Aspidotis (Sinopteridiaceae)
Small ferns. Divide as plants start into growth. H8

Asplenium (Aspleniaceae)
Ferns of varying sizes and qualities. Divide as growth starts. *A. bulbiferum* can be increased by leaf cuttings. H8

Astelia (Asteliaceae)
Dioecious perennials forming carpets or mounds. Sow fertile seed in spring. Divide following flowering. H8

Aster (Compositae)
Perennials of varying habits, sizes and quality. Sow fertile seed in spring. Divide as plants come into growth. Take stem cuttings of new growth in late spring or early summer. H7–9

Asteranthera ovata (Gesneriaceae)
Climbing sub-shrub for high rainfall areas. Sow seed in spring on chopped sphagnum moss. Take stem cuttings of non-flowering growth in late summer. H9

Asteriscus (Compositae)
Showy perennials, often short lived. Sow fertile seed in spring. Take stem cuttings of non-flowering growth if possible in late summer. H8–9

Astilbe (Saxifragaceae)
Perennials of varying sizes. Sow seed in spring. Divide as plants start into growth. H7–8

Astragalus (Leguminosae)
Annuals, perennials or sub-shrubs. Sow seed in spring after soaking in cold water for 24 hours. Take stem cuttings of non-flowering growth if possible in late summer. H9

Astrantia (Umbelliferae)
Perennials, most of which are rather large for a rock garden. Sow washed seed in spring. Divide as plants start into growth. H8

Astroloma (Epalidaceae)
Evergreen shrubs of varying sizes and habits. Sow seed in spring, germination is erratic. Take stem cuttings in autumn/fall, success variable. H9–10

Asyneuma (Campanulaceae)
Perennials of varying sizes and qualities. Sow seed in spring. Divide as plants start into growth. Take stem cuttings of new non-flowering growth in autumn/fall. H8

Athamanta (Umbelliferae)
Perennials. Sow seed in spring. Divide as plants start into growth. H8

Athyrium (Athyriaceae)
Ferns of varying sizes. Divide as plants start into growth. H8

Atractylis (Compositae)
Perennials of varying sizes and qualities. Sow seed in spring. H9

Atragene see *Clematis*

Atraphaxis (Polygonaceae)
Deciduous shrubs of varying sizes. Sow seed in spring. Take stem cuttings in late summer. H8

Aubrieta (Cruciferae)
Perennials. Sow seed in spring. Take cuttings of new growth in summer. H8

Aurina see *Alyssum*

Azorella (Umbelliferae)
Evergreen sub-shrub forming carpets, cushions or mounds. Sow seed in spring. Detach offsets when not in active growth. Take off newly formed rosettes and treat as cuttings. H8–9

Babiana (Iridaceae)
Winter-dormant corms. Sow seed in spring. Separate corms when dormant. H10

Baeckia (Myrtaceae)
Low-growing evergreen shrubs of varying habits and sizes. Sow seed in spring. Take stem cuttings of new growth in late summer. H9–10

91

Balaustion (Myrtaceae)
Small evergreen shrubs. Sow seed in spring. Take stem cuttings of new growth in autumn/fall. H10

Ballota (Labiatae)
Sub-shrubs of varying sizes. Sow seed in spring. Take stem cuttings of non-flowering growth in autumn/fall. H8

Balsamorrhiza (Compositae)
Rather large perennials, not easy to cultivate. Sow fertile seed in spring. Divide as plants start into growth. H8

Barnadesia (Compositae)
Deciduous shrubs of varying habits. Sow fertile seed in spring. Take stem cuttings of non-flowering growth in summer. H8

Barneoudia (Ranunculaceae)
Tuberous perennial. Sow seed in autumn/fall and expose to winter cold; germination can be delayed. Cut tuber into pieces at the end of dormant season; success variable. H8

Bartsia (Scrophulariaceae)
Annuals and perennials often short lived; these semi-parasites are difficult to cultivate. Sow seed sparingly in spring, do not separate seedlings before early planting. Success in establishment is variable. H8

Bauera rubioides (Baueraceae)
Evergreen shrub extremely variable in habit and size; select slow-growing prostrate alpine forms. Sow seed in spring. Take stem cuttings of new non-flowering growth in late summer. H9–10

Beauverdia see *Ipheion*

Begonia (Begoniaceae)
A very large genus of perennials, some of which are tuberous. Normally considered as warm glasshouse plants, a few are small enough and sufficiently hardy for a rock garden. Sow seed in spring. Tubers can be cut into pieces when dormant. Stem cuttings in late summer; leaf cuttings. Tubercles often form in leaf axils. H9–10

Bellendena montana (Proteaceae)
Evergreen shrub, not easy to cultivate. Sow fertile seed in spring; germination is erratic and often delayed. H9

Bellevalia see *Muscari*

Bellidastrum see *Aster*

Bellis (Compositae)
Perennials, and although *B. perennis* is a weed there is a number of highly desirable small-flowered forms which can be short lived. Sow seed in spring. Divide when not in active growth. H7

Bellium (Compositae)
Perennial which can be short lived. Sow seed in spring. Divide as plants start into growth. H8

Berberis (Berberidaceae)
Deciduous and evergreen spiny shrubs; although a large family only one or two species and/or cultivars are suited to a rock garden. Best germination is to autumn/fall sow seed after extracting from fruit and expose to winter cold. Take stem cuttings of deciduous kinds in summer, whilst the evergreens can be taken over a much longer period. H7–9

Bergenia (Saxifragaceae)
Perennials of varying sizes. Sow seed in spring. Divide when not in active growth; rhizomatous rootstock can be cut into pieces. H7–8

Bessera (Alliaceae)
Winter-dormant bulbs. Sow seed in spring. Separate bulbs when dormant. H9–10

Besseya (Scrophulariaceae)
Perennials, not easy to cultivate. Sow seed in spring when there is no immediate germination retain pot and expose to winter cold. H8

Betula nana (Betulaceae)
Probably the only species small enough to grow on a large rock garden. Seed, which should be moist stored, is autumn/fall sown and exposed to winter cold. Spring stem cuttings with a heel will sometimes root. H6

Biarum (Araceae)
Summer-dormant tubers. Sow seed in spring, although there is better germination if sown as soon as collected. Cut tubers into pieces when dormant. H9–10

Bidens (Compositae)
Annuals and perennials of varying habits and qualities; some are weeds. Sow seed in spring. Take stem cuttings in autumn/fall of non-flowering growth if possible. H9–10

Biebersteinia (Geraniaceae)
Tuberous perennial. Sow seed in spring. Divide tubers whilst dormant. H8–9

Biscutella (Cruciferae)
Perennials of varying qualities. Sow seed in spring. Take stem cuttings with a heel in summer; rooting can be erratic and delayed. Sometimes there is heavy callusing which prevents roots emerging; pare this away. H7–8

Blandfordia (Blandfordiaceae)
Perennial; each species is variable in size and hardiness, so the smallest and highest altitude forms should be chosen for a rock garden. Sow seed in spring. Success with division following flowering is variable. H9–10

Blechnum (Blechnaceae)
Ferns of varying sizes; *B. penna-marina* can be invasive in favourable localities. Divide as plants start into growth. H8–10

Bletia (Orchidaceae)
Terrestrial orchids. Divide following flowering. H9–10

Bletilla (Orchidaceae)
Beautiful terrestrial orchids, perhaps rather large for a rock garden. Divide following flowering. H9

Bloomeria (Alliaceae)
Bulbs. Sow seed in spring. Separate bulbs when dormant. H9–10

Blumenbachia (Loasaceae)
Although treated as annuals, these are short-lived showy perennials that have stinging hairs on their leaves. Sow seed in spring. H10

Boenninghausenia albiflora (Rutaceae)
Perennial or sub-shrub, variable in height and vigour. Sow seed in spring. Take stem cuttings of non-flowering growth in late spring or early summer. H9

Bolax see *Azorella*

Bommeria (Hemiontidaceae)
Ferns from hot dry areas that can be summer-dormant. Divide as they start into growth. H9

Bongardia (Berberidaceae)
Summer dormant tuberous perennials. Although seed can be spring sown there is better germination when sown immediately collected. Cut up tuber when dormant. H9–10

Boopis (Calyceraceae)
Some species which are or have been in this genus may be classified under *Nastanthus*. Perennials not easy to cultivate. Sow seed in spring. Stem cuttings taken in late summer may root but success is variable. H8

Borderia (Dioscoriaceae)
Tuberous perennials. Sow seed in spring. Divide whilst dormant. H9

Boronia (Rutaceae)
Evergreen, often intensely fragrant, small shrubs. Soak seed in boiling water for 24 hours before spring sowing. Take stem cuttings of new growth following flowering in late summer. H9–10

Botrychium (Ophioglossaceae)
Difficult ferns with separate sterile and fertile fronds. Divide as plants start into growth. H8–9

Bouvardia (Rubiaceae)
Small evergreen shrubs. Sow seed in spring. Stem cuttings of new growth in spring or early summer will root under mist or in a closed case. Prepare root cuttings in late autumn/fall. H9–10

Boykinia see *Telonix*

Brachycome (Compositae)
Annuals and perennials that are often short lived. Sow seed in spring. Take stem cuttings of non-flowering growth if possible in summer. H9

Brachyglottis (Compositae)
Evergreen shrubs of varying sizes. Sow fertile seed in spring. Take stem cuttings in autumn/fall of non-flowering growth. H8–9

Brassica balearica (Cruciferae)
Evergreen sub-shrub. Sow seed in spring. Take stem cuttings in autumn/fall. Prepare root cuttings in autumn/fall. H9

Bravoa (Amaryllidaceae)
(Species from this genus were formerly included in *Polianthes*.) Winter-dormant tuberous perennials. Sow seed in spring. Divide when not in active growth. H9

× *Briggandra calliantha* (*Briggsia aurantiaca* × *Opithandra primuloides*) (Gesneriaceae)
Perennial. Separate rosettes with roots when not in active growth. Make cuttings of newly developed mature leaves. H9

95

Briggsia (Gesneriaceae)
Perennial. Sow seed on chopped sphagnum moss in spring. Separate rooted rosettes when not in active growth. Take newly developed mature leaves as cuttings. H9

Brimeura see *Hyacinthus*

Brodiaea (Iridaceae)
Winter-dormant corms. Sow seed in spring. Separate corms when dormant. H9–10

Bruckenthalia spiculifolia (Ericaceae)
Small evergreen shrub. Sow seed on chopped sphagnum moss. Take stem cuttings of new growth as it begins to mature in late summer. H8

Brunonia australis (Brunoniaceae)
Showy annual. Sow seed in spring. H9

Bryanthus gmelinii (Ericaceae)
Low-growing or prostrate evergreen shrub; not easy. Sow seed on chopped sphagnum moss. Take stem cuttings of new maturing growth in late summer. H7

Bulbine (Asphodellaceae)
Perennials of varying sizes and qualities. Sow seed in spring. Separate or divide in spring as plants start into growth. H9–10

Bulbinella (Asphodellaceae)
Perennials of variable habit and size. Sow seed in spring. Divide following flowering. H8–9

Bulbocodium vernum (Colchicaceae)
Summer-dormant corm. Sow seed in spring. Separate corms when not in active growth. H8

Buphthalmum (Compositae)
Perennials variable in size. Sow seed in spring. Divide as plants come into growth. H8

Bupleurum (Umbelliferae)
Perennials and evergreen shrubs of varying sizes and habits. Sow seed in spring. Take stem cuttings of new non-flowering growth in autumn/fall. H8–9

Buxus (Buxaceae)
Evergreen shrubs which can become trees. *B. rugulosa* is small enough for a rock garden, as are some of the dwarf or prostrate cultivars of *B. sempervirens*.

Sow seed in spring. Take stem cuttings of mature growth in late autumn/fall or winter. H8

Caesia (Anthericaceae)
Perennials, not easy to cultivate. Sow seed in spring. Divide as plants come into growth. H10

Caiophora (Loasaceae)
Short-lived perennials, although they are treated as annuals; showy plants with stinging leaf hairs. Sow seed in spring. H10

Calamintha (Labiatae)
Aromatic perennials of differing vigour and quality. Sow seed in spring. Take stem cuttings of non-flowering growth in late summer. Divide at the end of winter. H8

Calandrinia (Portulacaceae)
Annuals and perennials that can be short lived. Sow seed in spring. H9–10

Calceolaria (Scrophulariaceae)
Annuals, perennials and evergreen shrubs of varying sizes. Sow seed in spring. Divide clump-formers in spring as they start into growth. Take stem cuttings of, if possible, non-flowering growth in autumn/fall. H8–10

Callianthemum (Ranunculaceae)
Perennials. Sow seed in autumn/fall so as to expose to winter cold. Germination can be erratic and delayed. H7

Callirrhoe (Malvaceae)
Rather large showy perennials. Sow seed in spring. Take stem cuttings in spring. H8–9

Calluna vulgaris (Ericaceae)
Low-growing extremely variable evergreen shrub of which some small cultivars may have a place on a rock garden. Take stem cuttings of new growth in summer. H7

Calocephalus (Compositae)
Small evergreen shrub. Sow seed in spring. Stem cuttings taken in late summer can root erratically. H10

Calochortus (Liliaceae)
Summer-dormant bulbs, many of which are difficult in cultivation. Fresh seed germinates best when spring sown; exposure to cold can stimulate germination of old seed. It is quite common after a good germination for the seedlings to

turn yellow and appear to die. This is natural die-back, leaving minuscule bulblets that need to be kept just moist. The easier species can be separated when not in active growth. H8–9.

Caltha (Ranunculaceae)
Perennials for a moist soil. Sow seed as fresh as possible, when germination can be quick. Older seed is erratic and long delayed; expose to winter cold. Divide following flowering. H6

Calycera (Calyceraceae)
Difficult perennials. Sow seed in spring. H8

Calydorea (Iridaceae)
Difficult but beautiful perennials. Sow seed in spring. H9–10

Calypso (Orchidaceae)
Beautiful but difficult terrestrial orchids. Divide following flowering. H8

Calypteridium (Portulacaceae)
Perennials. Sow seed in spring. H9

Campanula (Campanulaceae)
A large genus including annuals and perennials, some of which are monocarpic. Variable in size, habit and quality. Sow seed in spring. Take stem cuttings in late spring. Clump-formers can be divided as they come into growth. H7–10

Camptosorus (Aspleniaceae)
Fern, in which the tips of the fronds will root as they come in touch with the soil. H9

Campynema (Hypoxidaceae)
Difficult perennials. Sow seed in spring. H8

Cardamine (Cruciferae)
Annuals and perennials of varying qualitites, some of which can be weeds. Sow seed in spring. Divide following flowering. Weighing down the end of leaves with a stone so it is in touch with the soil before flowering will induce the leaf to produce a new plant in *C. pratensis* and occasionally with other species. *C. (Dentaria) bulbifera* produces tubercles in leaf axils. H7

Cardaminopsis (Cruciferae)
Perennials often short lived of varying sizes and qualities. Sow seed in spring. H7

Carduncellus (Compositae)
Perennials, some of which have monocarpic rosettes. Sow seed in spring. H8

Carex (Cyperaceae)
Perennials of varying sizes and qualities, of which a number of smaller New Zealand species recently introduced are proving to be attractive foliage plants. Sow seed in spring. Divide in spring. H6–8

Carlina (Compositae)
Perennial thistles. Sow seed in spring. Remove offsets after flowering. H8

Carmichaelia (Leguminosae)
Shrubs of varying sizes and habits. Sow seed in spring after soaking for 24 hours in boiling water. Take stem cuttings in autumn/fall. H8

Caryopteris (Verbenaceae)
Small deciduous shrubs suitable for a larger rock garden. Sow seed in spring. Take stem cuttings of new growth in late summer. There can be success with hardwood cuttings in winter. H8

Cassandra see *Chamaedaphne*

Cassiope (Ericaceae)
Small evergreen shrubs. Sow seed in spring on chopped sphagnum moss. Take stem cuttings of new non-flowering growth in autumn/fall. Division of established clumps as growth is starting is sometimes possible with varying results. H7

Castilleja (Scrophulariaceae)
Showy semi-parasites that are difficult to establish. Sow seed thinly in spring in small pots. Do not separate seedlings but plant the entire pot of seedlings into a permanent position whilst still small; success variable. H9

Catananche (Compositae)
Perennials, perhaps rather large for a rock garden. Sow seed in spring. Divide as plants start into growth. H8

Cathcartia see *Meconopsis*

Caulophyllum (Leontaceae/Berberidaceae)
Perennials. Although seed can be spring sown, there is better germination if sown as soon as seed is collected and exposed to winter cold. H8

Cautleya (Zingiberaceae)
Rhizomatous perennial. Sow seed in spring. Divide following flowering. H9

Ceanothus (Rhamnaceae)
Evergreen and deciduous shrubs, some of which can make trees. There are a few small or prostrate species and prostrate cultivars of normally larger ones that can be grown on a rock garden. Soak seed in boiling water for 24 hours before autumn/fall sowing and expose to winter cold; germination can be erratic and delayed. Take stem cuttings of evergreen species in autumn/fall. Stem cuttings of deciduous species root better if taken when soft in early summer. H8–10

Cedrus (Pinaceae)
Evergreen conifers that make very large trees but all species have produced small cultivars, some of which may find a place on a large rock garden. There can be success with wounded winter stem cuttings using bottom heat. Grafting may be necessary to ensure producing a miniature tree of typical habit. Use a side graft on a stock of the same species as the cultivar. H8

Celmisia (Compositae)
Rosette-forming perennials, some of which form mats. Sow fertile seed as soon as available for there is short viability. Although cold is not necesary for germination, it stimulates it. Divide established clumps following flowering. Take individual rosettes from carpeters and treat as cuttings. H8

Celsia see *Verbascum*

Centaurea (Compositae)
Annuals and perennials of varying sizes and qualities. Sow seed in spring. Divide in late winter. H7–8

Centaurium (Gentianaceae)
Annuals, biennials and perennials. Sow seed in spring. H8–9

Centrolepis (Centrolepidaceae)
Perennial cushion plant, not long lived. Sow fertile seed in spring. When cushions begin to fall apart, lift and pull to pieces when not in active growth. Carefully detach rooted portions from the circumference of younger plants, taking care not to spoil the symmetry. H9

Cerastium (Caryophyllaceae)
Perennials of varying qualities. Sow seed in spring. Take cuttings of new growth after flowering. Divide in early spring. H7–8

Ceratostigma (Plumbaginaceae)
Perennial and small deciduous shrubs. Sow seed in spring. Divide perennial as it comes into growth. Take soft cuttings of shrubby species in spring or early summer and root under mist or in a closed case. H8

Cephalotus follicularis (Cephalotaceae)
Perennial insectivorous plant for a moist soil. Sow seed in spring on chopped sphagnum moss. Divide as plants start into growth. H10

Ceterach (Aspleniaceae)
Small ferns. Divide when not in active growth. H7

Chaenactis (Compositac)
Perennials, often short lived. Sow seed in spring. Divide as plants come into growth. H8

Chaenorhinum (Scrophulariaceae)
Perennials. Sow seed in spring. Take stem cuttings of non-flowering growth in spring/early summer. To provide suitable growth for propagating, cut back a few shoots four weeks before propagating. H8

Chamaecyparis (Cupressaceae)
Large evergreen coniferous trees but most, probably all, species have produced small cultivars. Take stem cuttings in winter of current season's growth; wound and root over bottom heat. H7–9

Chamaecytisus (Leguminosae)
Evergreen shrubs of varying sizes and habits. Sow seed after soaking in boiling water for 24 hours. Take stem cuttings of non-flowering growth in autumn/fall. H9–10

Chamaedaphne calyculata (Ericaceae)
Small evergreen shrub. Sow seed on chopped sphagnum moss in spring. Take stem cuttings of new non-flowering growth in autumn/fall. H7

Chamaelirium luteum (Anthericaceae)
Tuberous perennial with usually dioecious flowers. Sow seed in spring. Separate or divide when dormant. H8

Chamaemelum (Compositae)
Aromatic perennials. Sow seed in spring. Take stem cuttings of non-flowering new growth in late summer. Lift and pull apart as growth is about to start. H8

Chamaenerion see *Epilobium*

Chamaepericlymenum see *Cornus*

Chamaescilla (Anthericaceae)
Small bulbs. Sow seed in spring. Separate when not in active growth. H9

Cheilanthes (Adiantaceae)
Ferns of varying sizes. Divide as they start into growth. H8–10

Cheiranthus (Cruciferaceae)
Perennials, the stems of which become woody with age, variable in size with most too large for a rock garden. Sow seed in spring. Take stem cuttings of non-flowering growth in late summer. H8–9

Chelidonium majus (Papaveraceae)
Short-lived perennial of little merit. Sow seed in spring; variants seem to come true from seed. H8

Chiastophyllum oppositifolium (Crassulaceae)
Succulent perennial. Sow seed in spring. Take stem cuttings of non-flowering growth in autumn/fall. H8

Chimaphila (Pyrolaceae)
Difficult perennials. Sow seed in autumn/fall as soon as ripe on chopped sphagnum moss and expose to winter cold; germination difficult. Division when not in active growth can be successful but more often fails. H7–8

Chiogenes see *Gaultheria*

Chionodoxa (Hyacinthaceae)
Summer dormant bulbs. Sow seed in spring. Separate bulbs when dormant. H7

Chionographis (Melanthiaceae)
Tuberous perennial. Sow seed in spring. Separate or divide when not in active growth. H8

Chionohebe (Scrophulariaceae)
Small evergreen sub-shrubs, most of which are cushions, but there is one species that is prostrate. Sow fertile seed in spring. Take off newly formed mature rosettes from outside of cushions and treat as cuttings. Take stem cuttings of *C. tetragona* in autumn/fall. H8

Chionophila jamesii (Scrophulariaceae)
Small perennial. Spring sow seed although exposure to winter cold stimulates germination. H8

Chirita (Gesneriaceae)
Perennial. Sow seed in spring on chopped sphagnum moss. Make cuttings of fully mature new leaves. H9–10

Chironia (Gentianaceae)
Perennials or small shrubs of varying sizes and habits. Sow seed in spring. Take stem cuttings of non-flowering growth in autumn/fall. H9–10

× *Chionoscilla* (*Chionodoxa lucilliae* × *Scilla bifolia*) (Hyacinthaceae)
Separate when dormant. Twin scaling. H7

Chorizema (Leguminosae)
Evergreen sprawlers or climbers. Sow seed in spring after soaking seed in boiling water for 24 hours. Take stem cuttings of non-flowering growth in spring. H10

Chrysanthemum (Compositae)
Only a few annuals now remain in this genus, most species have been transferred to other genera. Sow seed in spring. H8

Chrysobactron see *Bulbinella*

Chrysocoma (Compositae)
Small evergreen shrubs of varying sizes. Sow seed in spring. Take stem cuttings in autumn/fall. H10

Chrysogonum virginianum (Compositae)
Perennial. Sow seed in spring. Divide as growth starts in spring. H8

Chrysopsis (Compositae)
Usually low-growing spreading or mat-forming perennials. Sow seed in spring. Take early summer stem cuttings. H8

Chrysosplenium (Saxifragaceae)
Perennials for a moist soil. Sow seed in spring. Take stem cuttings in late summer of non-flowering growth. H8

Cichorium alpina (Compositae)
Spiny perennial, the stem of which can become woody with age. Sow fertile seed in spring. H8

Cipura (Iridaceae)
Winter-dormant corms. Sow seed in spring. Separate corms when dormant. H9

Cissus (Vitaceae)
Woody evergreen climbers or sprawlers of varying sizes, a few of which are small enough for a rock garden. Sow seed in spring. Take stem cuttings in autumn/fall. H10

Cistus (Cistaceae)
Evergreen shrubs of varying sizes and habits; often short lived. Sow seed in spring. Take stem cuttings of non-flowering new growth in early autumn/fall. H8–9

Claytonia (Portulacaceae)
Annuals, biennials and perennials of varying habits and qualities. Sow seed in spring, although autumn/fall sowing with exposure to winter cold gives better and more even germination. H7

Clarkia (Onagraceae)
Mostly annuals, but a few are short-lived perennials. Sow seed in spring. H8

Clematis (Ranunculaceae)
A large genus of mostly deciduous and evergreen climbers, but containing also perennials and shrubs. Probably only four are suited to a rock garden: *C. alpina, C. ochatensis, C. gentianoides* and *C. marmoraria*; the first two are monoecious and the last two dioecious. Sow fertile seed in spring; sometimes germination can be delayed when exposure to winter cold will help. Take internodal cuttings of the first three in late spring and root under mist or in a closed case; when cuttings have rooted and been potted they must be induced to make secondary growth before they go dormant. H7–9

Clintonia (Convallariaceae)
Perennials. Extract seed from fruit, wash and autumn/fall sow; germination can be long delayed. Divide as plants start into growth. H7

Cneorum (Cneoraceae)
Small evergreen shrubs. Sow seed in spring. Take stem cuttings of non-flowering growth in autumn/fall. H9

Codonopsis (Campanulaceae)
Perennials, many of which are sprawling or twiners, some are too large for a rock garden. Sow seed in spring. Take spring stem cuttings; success variable. H7–9

Colchicum (Colchicaceae)
Summer-dormant corms of which the spring leaves in many species are gross. Sow seed in spring. Separate corms when dormant. H8

Coleonema (Rutaceae)
Evergreen aromatic shrubs. Sow seed in spring. Take stem cuttings of non-flowering growth in autumn/fall. H9–10

104

Collomia (Polemoniaceae)
Annuals and perennials of varying sizes. Sow seed in spring. H7–8

Colobanthus (Caryophyllaceae)
Perennials of varying habits and qualities; those forming cushions are considered the best. Sow seed in spring. Carefully detach rooted pieces from the circumference without spoiling symmetry. H8

Commelina (Commelinaceae)
Perennials of varying sizes and habits. Sow seed in spring. Divide just before plants come into growth. H9

Conandron ramondioides (Gesneriaceae)
Winter dormant tuberous perennial. Sow seed in spring on chopped sphagnum moss. Cut tubers into pieces as new growth starts. Make cuttings of new mature leaves. H8

Conanthera (Tecophilaeaceae)
Winter dormant corms. Sow seed in spring. Separate corms when dormant. H9

Consolida (Ranunculaceae)
Annuals of varying sizes sometimes used for fillers. Spring sow seed. H8

Convallaria (Convallariaceae)
Winter dormant rhizomatous perennials. Extract seed from fruit. Wash and sow in autumn/fall; germination can be delayed. Divide whilst dormant in late winter. H7

Convolvulus (Convolvulaceae)
Annuals, perennials and shrubs of varying habits and qualities; some can be noxious weeds. Sow seed in spring. Clump formers can be divided as plants start into growth. Take late summer stem cuttings of non-flowering growth if possible. H8–9

Cooperia (Amaryllidaceae)
Bulb. Sow seed in spring. Separate bulbs when dormant; twin scaling. H9

Coprosma (Rubiaceae)
A large genus of mostly dioecious evergreen shrubs including trees. Grown for attractive fruits; some of the small prostrate kinds are suited to a rock garden. Extract seed from fruit, wash and spring sow. There are always more female than male seedlings, which are the last to germinate. It is preferable to sow very thinly, do not prick off but plant the pot of seedlings undisturbed. When seedlings flower, sex and label accordingly. Take stem cuttings of new growth in autumn/fall. H8–10

105

Coptis (Ranunculaceae)
Perennials. Autumn/fall sow seed and expose to winter cold; germination can be delayed. Divide clumps as they pass out of flower. H7

Cordyline (Agavaceae)
Evergreen trees or shrubs of which *C. pumilo* could find a place on a larger rock garden. Sow seed in spring. H9

Coreopsis (Compositae)
Perennials better suited to herbaceous border but some of the smaller could find a place on a rock garden. Sow fertile seed in spring. Divide as plants start into growth. H8

Corethrogyne (Compositae)
Perennials, the stems of which can become woody with age. Sow seed in spring. Take stem cuttings of non-flowering growth in summer. H9

Coris (Primulaceae)
Low-growing perennials, the stems of which can become woody with age. Sow seed in spring. Take non-flowering stem cuttings in late summer. H9

Cornus (Cornaceae)
Deciduous trees and shrubs of which possibly only *C. canadensis* and *C. sueica* are suited to a rock garden; plants are self-sterile. Autumn/fall sow seed after extracting from fruit and washing. Divide as plants come into growth. H6

Coronilla (Leguminosae)
Perennials and evergreen shrubs of varying sizes and habits. Spring sow seed after soaking for 24 hours in cold water. Take stem cuttings of new growth in summer. H9

Corokia cotoneaster (Cornaceae)
Self-sterile evergreen shrub with divaricating habit variable in size. Sow washed seed in spring. Take stem cuttings of non-flowering growth in late summer. H9

Correa (Rutaceae)
Evergreen shrubs of varying size and habits. Sow seed in spring. Take stem cuttings of non-flowering growth in late summer. H9–10

Cortusa (Primulaceae)
Perennials, often short lived. Sow seed in spring. H8

Corybas (Orchidaceae)
Difficult small terrestrial orchids. Divide following flowering. H9–10

Corydalis (Fumariaceae)
Annuals, also perennials which often die down early; some are tuberous. Sow seed in spring. Divide perennials as they go out of flower. Lift tubers when dormant and cut into pieces. H7–9

Cotoneaster (Rosaceae)
Deciduous and evergreen shrubs that can make trees. Some of the smallest or prostrate forms or species are suited to a larger rock garden. Sow seed in autumn/fall after extracting from fruit and washing. Take stem cuttings of non-fruiting growth in late summer. H7–8

Cotula (Compositae)
Low-growing or creeping perennials of varying vigour and quality. Sow fertile seed in spring. Many plants root as they grow so that rooted pieces can be detached at most times. Take stem cuttings in late summer of non-flowering growth if this is possible. H8

Cotyledon (Crassulaceae)
Perennials or evergreen succulent shrubs of varying sizes. Sow fertile seed in spring, although it is better to sow immediately collected. Stem or leaf-bud cuttings can be taken in late summer. H8–10

Craspedia (Compositae)
Tufted perennials, can be short lived. Sow fertile seed in spring. Some lend themselves to division as plants start into growth. H8–9

Crassula (Crassulaceae)
Annuals, perennials and shrubs of varying sizes and qualities. Sow seed in spring. Divide perennials as they come into growth. Take stem cuttings of non-flowering growth if possible in late summer. H9

Craterocaspa (Campanulaceae)
Difficult perennials. Sow seed in spring. H8

Craterostigma (Scrophulariaceae)
Difficult perennials. Sow seed in spring. H8

Cremanthodium (Compositae)
Perennials that are often difficult to keep. Sow seed in spring. Division in early spring is possible with stoloniferous species. H8

Crepis (Compositae)
Perennials of differing qualities. Sow seed in spring. Divide as plants start into growth. H7–8

Crocopsis (Amaryllidaceae)
Bulbs. Sow seed in spring. Separate bulbs when dormant. H9

Crocosmia (Iridaceae)
Winter-dormant corms, some of which are rather large for a rock garden; *C.* × *crocosmiflora* can become a weed. Sow seed in spring. Separate corms when dormant. H8

Crocus (Iridaceae)
Summer-dormant corms. Sow seed in spring. Separate when dormant. H7–8

Crowea (Rutaceae)
Small evergreen shrubs of variable habit. Sow seed in spring. Take stem cuttings of non-flowering growth in autumn/fall. H9–10

Crucinella see *Phuyopsis*

Cruckshankia (Rubiaceae)
Difficult perennials. Sow seed in spring. Take stem cuttings of non-flowering growth in late summer. H8

Cryptogramma (Cryptogrammataceae/Adiantaceae)
Ferns. Divide when not in active growth. H8

Cryptomeria japonica (Taxodiaceae)
Coniferous forest tree that has produced small cultivars. Take winter stem cuttings and root, if possible, over bottom heat. H7

Ctenitis (Aspidiaceae)
Ferns of varying sizes. Divide when not in active growth. H8

Culcitium (Compositae)
Difficult perennial. Sow fertile seed in spring. H8

Cunila (Labiatae)
Aromatic perennials of varying sizes and habits. Sow seed in spring. Take stem cuttings of new growth in spring. H8

Cuphea (Lythraceae)
Showy perennials of varying sizes and habits. Sow seed in spring. Take stem cuttings of non-flowering shoots if possible in autumn/fall. H9–10

Cupressus (Cupressaceae)
Evergreen coniferous trees and large shrubs, of which *C. pygmaea* is the only species suited to a rock garden, although most species have produced small

cultivars. Sow seed of *C. pygmaea* in spring. Take stem cuttings in winter, wound and root if possible, over bottom heat. H8–9

Cyananthus (Campanulaceae)
Choice small perennials. Sow seed in spring. Divide growth. H8

Cyanella (Tecophilaeaceae)
Summer-dormant corms. Sow seed in spring. Separate corms when dormant. H9

Cyathodes (Epacridaceae)
Often dioecious evergreen shrubs of which New Zealand species are easier to grow than those from Australia. Extract seed from fruit and sow as fresh as possible; germination often difficult. Take stem cuttings of new growth as it begins to mature in late summer; success variable. H8–9

Cyclamen (Primulaceae)
Tuberous perennial. Best germination is from sowing freshly collected seed. When sowing in spring or using old seed, soak for 24 hours in plenty of cold water. Germination can be delayed. H8–10

Cyclobothra see *Calochortus*

Cymbalaria (Scrophulariaceae)
Sprawling perennials that can be weeds. Sow seed in spring. Take cuttings if possible of non-flowering growth in late summer. H8

Cymbidium (Orchidaceae)
Epiphytic and terrestrial orchids usually grown in glasshouses, but a few terrestrials are small enough for a rock garden. Divide following flowering. H9–10

Cynoglossum (Boraginaceae)
Showy annuals, biennials and perennials, often short lived and rather large for rock gardens. Sow seed in spring. H8

Cypella (Iridaceae)
Corms. Sow seed in spring. Separate corms when dormant. H9

Cypripedium (Orchidaceae)
Beautiful terrestrial orchids. Divide immediately following flowering. H8

Cyrtandra (Gesneriaceae)
Shrubs of varying sizes. Sow seed in spring on chopped sphagnum moss. Take stem cuttings of non-flowering growth in autumn/fall. H9–10

109

Cyrtanthus (Amaryllidaceae)
Bulbs of varying sizes. Sow seed in spring. Separate bulbs when dormant; twin scaling. H9–10

Cyrtomium (Aspidiaceae)
Ferns of varying sizes. Divide established clumps with multiheads as they come into growth. H9

Cystopteris (Anthyriaceae)
Ferns of varying sizes. Divide whilst dormant. *C. bulbifera* can be increased by leaf cuttings. H7–8

Cytisus (Leguminosae)
Evergreen or deciduous shrubs of varying sizes and habits. Sow seed after soaking for 24 hours in cold water in spring. Take short stem cuttings with a heel in late summer. H8

Daboecia (Ericaceae)
Small evergreen shrubs. Sow seed in spring on chopped sphagnum moss. Take stem cuttings in late summer of new growth. H8

Dacrydium laxifolium see *Lepidothamnus laxifolius*

Dactylorhiza (Orchidaceae)
Terrestrial orchids. Divide immediately after flowering. H8

Daiswa see *Paris*

Dalibarda see *Rubus*

Dampiera (Coodeniaceae)
Difficult perennials of varying sizes and habits. Sow seed in spring. H10

Danae racemosa (Ruscaceae)
Evergreen shrub perhaps too large for a rock garden. Autumn/fall sow seed and expose to winter cold; germination can be erratic and delayed. Division in early spring may be possible on established clumps. H8

Daphne (Thymelaeaceae)
Evergreen and deciduous shrubs of varying sizes and habits. Sow washed seed after extraction from fruit in autumn/fall and expose to winter cold for best germination. Take stem cuttings of evergreens, which are easier to root, in late summer. The less easy deciduous species give better results when using soft new growth under mist or in a closed case. *D. mezerum* and *D. gwenka* can be increased from root cuttings taken in late autumn/fall. Low growing and

spreading species, e.g. *D. cneorum* and *D. blageana* can be layered in late summer. *D. petraea* and its selections are often grafted because it is said to produce longer-lived plants. This and others, especially deciduous kinds which are difficult from cuttings, can be grafted onto seedling *D. mezereum* in late winter using a cleft graft. H8–9

Darlingtonia californica (Sarraceniaceae)
Insectivorous pitcher plant. Sow seed on chopped sphagnum moss as soon as it is collected. Divide as plants come into growth. H9–10

Darwinia (Myrtaceae)
Evergreen shrubs of varying sizes and habits. Sow seed in spring. Take stem cuttings of non-flowering growth in autumn/fall. H10

Davallia (Davalliaceae)
Epiphytic fern. Separate rhizome when dormant; cut rhizomes into pieces when dormant. H8–10

Deinanthe (Hydrangeaceae)
Perennials. Sow seed in spring. Divide as plants start into growth. H8

Delphinium (Ranunculaceae)
Annuals and perennials of varying sizes. Sow seed in spring; if germination is delayed expose to winter cold. Divide established clumps as they come into growth. Take stem cuttings of soft new growth in spring. H7–9

Dendrobium (Orchidaceae)
Epiphytic and terrestrial orchids of which one or two are suited to a rock garden. Divide immediately after flowering. H9–10

Dentaria see *Cardamine*

Deutzia gracilis (Hydrangeaceae)
Some of the selections of this species may be small enough for a rock garden. Take stem cuttings in late summer. H8

Dianella (Phormiaceae)
Evergreen perennials of varying sizes and qualities. Sow seed extracted from fruit in spring. Divide as plants start into growth. Some have a suckering habit. On occasions plantlets can be produced on the inflorescence; treat these as cuttings. H9

Dianthus (Caryophyllaceae)
A large genus of annuals and perennials of varying sizes, habits and qualities. Sow seed in spring. Take stem cuttings of non-flowering growth in late summer. Some clump formers can be divided as they come into growth. H8–9

111

Diapensia (Diapensiaceae)
Prostrate evergreen shrubs, difficult. Sow seed in spring on chopped sphagnum moss. Take stem cuttings of non-flowering growth in late summer or early autumn/fall. H6

Diascia (Scrophulariaceae)
Self-sterile annuals and perennials that can be short lived. Sow fertile seed in spring. Divide established clumps in spring. Take cuttings of non-flowering growth in autumn/fall; cut back half of plant to produce suitable growth. H8–9

Dicentra (Fumariaceae/Papaveraceae)
Perennials of varying sizes and qualities. For best germination, sow seed as soon as it is ripe. Divide as plants come into growth. H8

Dichelostemma (Alliaceae)
Winter-dormant bulbs, perhaps rather large for a rock garden. Sow seed in spring. Separate bulbs when dormant. H9–10

Dicranostigma (Papaveraceae)
Annuals and perennials, often short lived. Sow seed in spring. H8

Dictyolimon macrorhabdos (Plumbaginaceae)
Biennial or short-lived perennial. Sow seed in spring. H8–9

Dierama (Iridaceae)
Evergreen corms, mostly too large for a rock garden. Sow seed in spring. Separate corms when not in active growth. H8

Digitalis (Scrophulariaceae)
Annuals, biennials and perennials of varying sizes, often short lived. Sow seed in spring. H7–9

Dimorphotheca see *Osteospermum*

Dionaea muscipula (Droseraceae)
Insectivorous perennial. Sow seed in spring on chopped sphagnum. H9–10

Dionysia (Primulaceae)
Evergreen perennial with most species forming tight cushions that need skilled protected cultivation. Sow seed in spring. Divide clump-formers at their most dormant. From the cushion species detach rosettes when newly formed from the circumference and treat as a cutting. H8

Diosphaera (Campanulaceae)
Perennials forming mats or loose cushions. Sow seed in spring. Detach rooted pieces if they occur. Take stem cuttings in autumn/fall. H9

Diotis see *Otanthus*

Dipcadi (Hyacinthaceae)
Winter-dormant bulb. Sow seed in spring. Separate bulbs when dormant. H9

Dipidax (Colchicaceae)
Bulb. Sow seed in spring. Separate bulbs when not in active growth. H10

Diplarrhena (Iridaceae)
Perennial. Sow seed in spring. Divide established clumps as they start into growth. H8–9

Disporum (Convallariaceae)
Perennial. Sow seed in autumn/fall and expose to winter cold; germination erratic and can be delayed. Divide established clumps as they start into growth. H7

Dodecatheon (Primulaceae)
Perennials that can be short lived. Sow seed in spring. Divide established clumps as they start into growth. H8–9

Dolichoglottis scorzonerioides (Compositae) (Formerly *Senecio scorzonerioides.*)
Perennial. Sow fertile seed in spring. Divide established clumps as they start into growth. H8

Donatia novae-zelandica (Donatiaceae)
Difficult cushion-forming sub-shrub. Sow fertile seed in spring on chopped sphagnum moss. Detach newly formed rosettes from perimeter of cushion and treat as cuttings; not easy. H8

Dondia see *Hacquetia*

Doronicum (Compositae)
Although botanical alpines, these perennials are too large for a rock garden. Sow seed in spring. Divide following flowering. H7

Dorycnium (Leguminosae)
Evergreen shrubs of varying sizes and quality. Sow seed in spring after soaking in cold water for 24 hours. Take cuttings of non-flowering growth in autumn/fall. H8

Douglasia (Primulaceae)
(*D. vitallina* and on occasions other species may be classified under *Androsace.*) Perennials forming loose cushions or mats. Sow seed in spring. Take

stem cuttings in late summer. Detach newly formed rosettes and treat as cuttings. H7–8

Draba (Cruciferae)
Annuals and perennials some forming cushions; others can be weedy. Sow seed in spring. Divide clump-forming species when not in active growth. Take off newly developed rosettes from circumference of cushions and treat as cuttings. H7–8

Dracocephalum (Labiatae)
Perennials of varying sizes. Sow seed in spring. Take stem cuttings of non-flowering growth in summer. Divide as plants start into growth. H8–9

Dracophyllum (Epacridaceae)
Evergreen shrubs of varying sizes and habits including carpeters and cushions; not easy. Sow fertile seed as fresh as possible on sphagnum moss; germination is difficult and erratic. Stem cuttings taken in late summer can sometimes be induced to root. No one has yet succeeded in vegetative propagation of cushion-forming *D. minimum*. H9

Drapetes (Thymeliaceae)
Evergreen sub-shrubs, some of which form cushions. Sow fertile seed in spring. Take cuttings of non-flowering growth in late summer. H9

Drosera (Droseraceae)
Annual and perennial instectivorous plants. Sow seed of bog species in spring on chopped sphagnum moss. Australian species that come from drier areas can be sown on an ordinary lime-free seed compost. H7–9

Droserophylum lusitanica (Droseraceae)
Insectivorous perennial the stem of which becomes woody with age. Sow seed in spring. H9

Dryas (Rosaceae)
Prostrate evergreen sub-shrub. Sow seed in autumn/fall and expose to winter cold. Take stem cuttings of non-flowering growth in autumn/fall. H6

Drymophila (Convallariaceae)
Perennial. Sow seed after extraction from fruit; germination difficult and erratic. Divide established clumps as they come into growth. H9

Dryopteris (Aspidiaceae)
Ferns of varying sizes and qualities. Divide when not in active growth. H7

Drypis spinosa (Aryophyllaceae)
Spiny perennial. Sow seed in spring. Divide as plants start into growth. H8–9

Duchesnia (Rosaceae)
Perennials of little merit. Sow seed taken from fruit in autumn/fall. Plant increases naturally by runners. H7

Dudleya (Crassulaceae)
Perennials with succulent rosettes. Sow seed in spring. Detach offsets in autumn/fall. H10

Duvalia (Asclepidaceae)
Somewhat succulent perennials of varying habits. Sow seed in spring. Take stem cuttings in late summer. H10

Ebenus (Leguminosae)
Perennials or evergreen sub-shrubs. Sow seed in spring after soaking for 24 hours in boiling water. Take stem cuttings in autumn/fall; success variable. H9

Echeandia (Anthericaceae)
Bulbs, perhaps too large for all but the largest rock gardens. Sow seed in spring. Separate bulbs when not in active growth. H9–10

Echeveria (Crassulaceae)
Perennials composed of succulent rosettes. Sow seed in spring. Detach offsets in autumn/fall.

Echinospartium (Leguminosae)
Evergreen spiny small shrubs. Sow seed in spring after soaking for 24 hours in boiling water. H9

Edraianthus (Campanulaceae)
Biennials and perennials with a tufted habit, often short lived. Sow seed in spring. Divide clumps as they start into growth. H9

Elmera racemosa (Saxifragaceae)
Perennial. Whilst seed can be spring sown, there seems to be better germination when autumn/fall sown and exposed to cold. Divide established clumps as they start into growth. H8

Eminium (Araceae)
Summer-dormant tuber. Although seed can be spring sown, the best germination is when sown as fresh as possible. Cut tubers into pieces when dormant. H9

115

Empetrum (Empetraceae)
Evergreen sub-shrubs that are usually dioecious. Sow seed when extracted from fruit in autumn/fall and expose to winter cold. Take stem cuttings of non-fruiting growth in autumn/fall. H7

Enargia see **Luzuriaga**

Eomecon (Papaveraceae)
Perennials with underground storage organ. Sow seed in spring. Divide or cut up when dormant. H8

Epacris (Epacridaceae)
Evergreen shrubs of varying sizes which are dioecious. Sow fertile seed when extracted from fruit in spring; germination can be difficult and erratic. Take stem cutting of new mature growth in late summer from young stock plants; success variable. H9–10

Ephedra (Ephedraceae)
Shrubs of variable habit that are dioecious. Sow seed in spring after extracting from fruit. Pull apart established clumps in early spring. H7–8

Epigaea (Ericaceae)
Evergreen sub-shrubs. Sow seed in spring on chopped sphagnum moss. Take stem cuttings of new growth in late summer. H8

Epilobium (Onagraceae)
Perennials of varying sizes and quality; some are invasive and a number are weeds. Sow seed in spring. Divide when dormant. H7–8

Epimedium (Berberidaceae)
Self-sterile perennials. Sow seed in spring. Divide when dormant. H8

Epipactis (Orchidaceae)
Terrestrial orchids. Divide following flowering. H8

Eranthis (Ranunculaceae)
Summer-dormant tuberous perennials. Sow seed immediately it is ripe and expose to winter cold. Separate tubers when not in active growth. H8

Eremia (Ericaceae)
Small evergreen shrubs. Sow seed on chopped sphagnum moss in spring. Take stem cuttings in late summer. H10

116

Eremostachys (Labiatae)
Perennials of varying sizes. Sow seed in spring. H8

Erica (Ericaceae)
Evergreen shrubs of varying sizes. Sow seed in spring on chopped sphagnum moss. Take stem cuttings of new non-flowering growth in summer. H7–10

Erigeron (Compositae)
A large genus of perennials of varying sizes and qualities; some are weedy. Sow fertile seed in spring. Clump-formers can be divided as they start into growth. Many can be increased by taking stem cuttings in autumn/fall. H7–8

Erinacea anthyllis (Leguminosae)
Spiny shrub. Sow fertile seed after soaking in cold water for 24 hours. Take short stem cuttings with a heel of mature growth in late summer; success variable. H8

Erinus (Scrophulariaceae)
Perennial. Sow seed in spring. Divide as plants start into growth. H8

Eriogonum (Polygonaceae)
Perennials that can form tight mats, almost cushions, and sub-shrubs. Sow seed in spring. Take stem cuttings in late summer. Some can be divided as they start into growth. H7–9

Eriophorum (Cyperaceae)
Moisture-loving perennials that can be difficult in cultivation. Sow fertile seed on chopped sphagnum moss in spring. Divide as plants start into growth. H6

Eriophyllum (Compositae)
Perennials. Sow fertile seed in spring. Divide established clumps as they start into growth. Take stem cuttings of non-flowering growth in late summer. H8

Eriostemon (Rutaceae)
Evergreen shrubs of varying sizes. Sow seed in spring. Take late-summer stem cuttings of non-flowering growth. H9–10

Eritrichium (Boraginaceae)
Perennials that are difficult to keep. Sow seed in spring. H8

Erodium (Geraniaceae)
Perennials. Sow seed in spring. Divide clumps in spring or detach pieces from multi-headed crowns. Take stem cuttings of non-flowering growth in late summer. Take root cuttings in late autumn/fall. H8–9

117

Eryngium (Umbelliferae)
Evergreen perennials of varying sizes. Sow seed in spring. Divide established clumps in spring as they start into growth; success variable. Take root cuttings in late autumn/fall; success variable. H8–9

Erysimum (Cruciferae)
(Including some species previously in *Cheiranthus*.) Perennials that can become woody with age; of varying sizes, habits and qualities. Sow seed in spring. Take stem cuttings of non-flowering growth in late summer. H8–9

Erythraea see *Centaurium*

Erythronium (Liliaceae)
Summer-dormant bulbs. Sow seed in spring. Lift bulbs (which in the garden can be very deep) when dormant, and separate. H8

Escallonia minima (Escalloniaceae)
Evergreen shrub. Sow seed in spring. Take stem cuttings of non-flowering growth in autumn/fall. H9

Eschscholtzia (Papaveraceae)
Annuals and perennials that can be short lived. Sow seed in spring. H8–9

Eucomis (Hyacinthaceae)
Winter-dormant bulbs, most of which are too big for a rock garden. Sow seed in spring. Separate bulbs when dormant; bulb cuttage or twin scaling. H8–9

Eunomia see *Aethionema*

Euonymus (Celastraceae)
Evergreen and deciduous shrubs most of which are too large for a rock garden. Sow seed in spring. Take stem cuttings in autumn/fall. H7–9

Euphorbia (Euphorbiaceae)
A very large genus including annuals, perennials and shrubs, many of which are succulent; of varying sizes, habits and qualities. Sow seed in spring. Take stem cuttings in late summer; after preparation leave for an hour until the latex dries before inserting. Rooting is better on an open bench. H7–10

Euphrasia (Scrophulariaceae)
A large genus of perennial semi-parasites, many of which are most attractive. All are difficult to cultivate. Sow seed thinly in spring. On germination do not disturb, and plant out pots of seedlings into their permanent position; success variable. H8

Euryops (Compositae)
Evergreen shrubs of varying sizes. Sow fertile seed in spring. Take stem cuttings of non-flowering growth in autumn/fall. H8–10

Eustephia (Amaryllidaceae)
Bulbs. Sow seed in spring. Separate when not in active growth. H9

Eustoma (Gentianaceae)
Perennials of varying sizes. Sow seed in spring. H9–10

Ewartia (Compositae)
Mat-forming perennials. Sow fertile seed in spring. Take off newly formed rosettes as cuttings in late summer. H8

Exacum (Gentianaceae)
Annuals, biennials or short-lived perennials. Sow seed in spring. H9–10

Fabiana (Solanaceae)
Evergreen shrubs of varying sizes and habits. Sow seed in spring. Take stem cuttings in autumn/fall of non-flowering growth. H9

Felicia (Compositae)
Annuals, perennials and shrubs of varying sizes, habits and qualities. Sow seed in spring. Take stem cuttings of non-flowering growth in late summer. H8–10

Ferraria (Iridaceae)
Winter-dormant bulbs. Sow seed in spring. Separate bulbs when dormant. H9

Fibigia (Cruciferae)
Perennials, the stem-bases of which can become woody with age. Sow seed in spring. H8

Ficus pumila (Moraceae)
Self-clinging woody climber. Sow seed in spring. Take stem cuttings when not in active growth. H10

Forstera (Stylidiaceae)
Mat-forming perennial that can be difficult. Sow fertile seed on chopped sphagnum moss in spring. Detach rooted pieces if available or take off loose rosettes and treat as cuttings during the summer. H9

Forsythia '**Arnolds Dwarf**' (Oleaceae)
Deciduous shrub, perhaps a little large for a rock garden. Take stem cuttings in summer, autumn/fall or winter. H7

119

Fortunata (Hyacinthaceae)
Winter-dormant bulb. Sow seed in spring. Separate bulbs when dormant; twin scaling. H9–10

Fragaria (Rosaceae)
Perennials of varying qualities. Sow seed in autumn/fall. Take off rooted runners in autumn/fall. H7–8

Francoa sonchifolia (Saxifragaceae)
Perennial. Sow seed in spring. H9

Frankenia (Frankeniaceae)
Perennials or sub-shrubs. Sow seed in spring. Take stem cuttings of non-flowering growth in late summer. H8

Frasera (Gentianaceae)
(Species of this genus can appear under *Gentiana or Swertia.*) Perennials that can be short lived. Sow seed in spring. H8

Freesia (Iridaceae)
Summer-dormant bulbs. Sow seed in spring. Separate bulbs when dormant. H10

Fritillaria (Liliaceae)
Bulbs (*Korolkowia* and *Rhinopetalum* are sometimes included with Fritillaria). Most seed ought to germinate if spring sown; if not expose to winter cold. Separate bulbs when dormant. Species where there are two large scales can be divided. Gather 'rice' and sow as though large seeds after soaking for 24 hours in cold water. Species that have large bulbs can be increased by taking off a few of the outer scales. H7–9

Fuchsia (Onagraceae)
Deciduous or evergreen trees or shrubs of varying sizes and habits. The most common in cultivation, *F. magellanica*, has produced small cultivars and there is a range of so-called hardy fuchsias of small stature of hybrid origin with this species. Sow seed of the species after extracting from fruit in spring. Stem cuttings taken at almost any season will root; avoid flowers if possible. H8–10

Fumana (Cistaceae)
Small evergreen shrubs. Sow seed in spring. Take stem cuttings of non-flowering growth in late summer. H9

Fumaria (Fumariaceae)
Annuals and short-lived perennials of varying qualities. Sow seed in spring. H8

120

Gagea (Liliaceae)
Winter-dormant bulbs but, with the exception of *G. lutea*, not easy. Sow seed in spring. Separate bulbs when dormant. H8–9

Galanthus (Amaryllidaceae)
Summer-dormant bulbs. Sow seed in spring, although there is better germination if sown immediately it is ripe. Separate bulbs immediately following flowering. Twin scaling when bulbs are dormant. H7

Galax (Diapensiaceae)
Perennial. Sow seed on chopped sphagnum moss in spring. Divide as plants come into growth. H7

Galaxia (Iridaccac)
Winter-dormant corms. Sow seed in spring. Separate corms when dormant. H9

Galium (Rubiaceae)
Annuals and perennials of varying qualities, some are weeds. Sow seed in spring. Divide as they start into growth. H7

× *Gaulnettya* (Ericaceae)
Evergreen shrubs. Bigeneric hybrids between various species of *Gaultheria* and *Pernettya*. Take stem cuttings in late summer. H8

Gaultheria (Ericaceae)
Evergreen shrubs of varying sizes and habits. Sow seed on chopped sphagnum moss in spring. Take stem cuttings in late summer. Prostrate species often root as they grow; some of the clump formers can be divided as they start into growth. H7–9

Gaylussacia (Ericaceae)
Deciduous shrubs of varying sizes. Sow seed on chopped sphagnum moss in spring. Take stem cuttings from mid to late summer. H7–8

Gazania (Compositae)
Perennials of varying qualities. Sow fertile seed in spring. Take stem cuttings in autumn/fall, many of which will almost certainly have flowers. H10

Geissorhiza (Iridaceae)
Winter-dormant corms. Sow seed in spring. Separate corms when dormant. H8–9

Gelasine azurea (Iridaceae)
Corm, perhaps rather large for a rock garden. Sow seed in spring. Separate corms when dormant. H9

Genista (Leguminosae)
Evergreen or deciduous shrubs, often spiny, of varying sizes and habits. Sow seed in spring after soaking for 24 hours in cold water. Take stem cuttings with a heel in autumn/fall. H8–9

Gentiana (Gentianaceae)
A large genus of perennials of varying sizes. Sow seed as fresh as possible in autumn/fall and expose to winter cold; germination can be delayed. Divide spring flowerers after blooming and autumn/fall bloomers in spring. Take stem cuttings of autumn bloomers in early summer and the soft new growth of spring flowerers after blooming. H6–9

Gentianella (Gentianaceae)
Annuals, biennials and short-lived perennials. Many species of former *Gentiana* are now included in this genus. Autumn/fall sow seed. H7–8

Gentianopsis (Gentianaceae)
Difficult perennials. Some species formerly in *Gentiana* may now appear here. Sow seed in autumn/fall. Divide as plants start into growth. H7–8

Geranium (Geraniaceae)
A large genus of perennials of varying habits, sizes and qualities. Sow seed in spring. Take stem cuttings of non-flowering growth in summer. Divide clump-formers in spring as they start into growth. Many species can be raised from root cuttings taken in autumn/fall. H7–9

Geum (Rosaceae)
Perennials of varying sizes and qualities. Sow seed in autumn/fall and expose to winter cold. Divide established clumps as they come into growth. Take stem cuttings of non-flowering growth in autumn/fall. H7–8

Gilia (Polemoniaceae)
Annuals, biennials and perennials, often short lived. Species formerly in this genus may now be found in *Ipomopsis* or *Linanthus*. Sow seed in spring. H8

Gilliesia (Alliaceae)
Winter-dormant bulbs. Sow seed in spring. Separate when dormant. H9

Gladiolus (Iridaceae)
Corms of varying sizes of which only a few are small enough for a rock garden. Sow seed in spring. Separate corms when dormant. H8–9

Glandularia see *Verbena*

Glaucidium palmatum (Paeoniaceae/Papaveraceae/Glaucidiaceae)
Perennial. Sow seed as fresh as possible in autumn/fall and expose to winter's cold. Divide established clumps as they start into growth. H7

Glaucium (Papaveraceae)
Annuals or short lived perennials. Sow seed in spring. H8–9

Glaux maritima (Primulaceae)
Perennial. Sow seed in spring. Separate in early spring. H8

Glechoma see *Nepeta*

Gleichenia (Gleicheniaceae)
Evergreen ferns not easy to cultivate. Divide as plants come into growth. H8–9

Globularia (Globulariaceae)
Perennials or sub-shrubs. Sow seed in spring. Take stem cuttings of new growth after flowering in late summer. H8

Gnaphalium (Compositae)
Annuals and perennials of varying habits, sizes and qualities; many are weedy. Sow seed in spring. Divide clump formers as they start into growth. Take stem cuttings of non-flowering growth in autumn/fall. H7–8

Goodenia (Goodeniaceae)
Perennials of varying sizes, only a few of which are small enough for a rock garden. Sow seed in spring. Take stem cuttings in autumn/fall. H9–10

Goodyera (Orchidaceae)
Terrestrial orchids with handsome leaves which can be difficult to establish. Divide following flowering. H7–8

Grammitis (Gramitidaceae)
Ferns often epiphytic. Divide as they start into growth. H8

Gratiola (Scrophulariaceae)
Annuals and perennials of varying sizes. Sow seed in spring, although when autumn/fall sown there is better germination. Take autumn/fall stem cuttings. Divide in early spring. H8

Greenovia (Crassulaceae)
Succulent rosette-forming perennials. Sow seed in spring. Detach off-sets in autumn/fall. H10

Grevillea (Proteaceae)
Evergreen trees and shrubs of varying sizes, only a few of which are small enough for a rock garden. Sow seed in spring after soaking for 24 hours in cold water; germination is erratic and can be delayed. Take stem cuttings of non-flowering growth in autumn/fall. H9–10

123

Gunnera (Haloragaea Gunneraceae)
Perennials of varying sizes, usually dioecious, suitable for a moist soil. The best-known species, *G. manicata* and *G. chilensis*, are the exceptions in being giants; most are small. Sow fertile seed immediately after extraction from fruits; although not essential, cold stimulates germination. Divide as clumps come into growth. H8–10

Gymnadenia (Orchidaceae)
Terrestrial orchid. Divide immediately after flowering. H8

Gymnocarpium (Aspleniaceae)
Small ferns. Divide as they come into growth. H8

Gymnopteris (Adiantaceae)
Small ferns. Divide as they start into growth. H8

Gymnospermium (Berberidaceae/Leonticaceae)
Summer-dormant tubers. Spring-sown seed will germinate but there are better results from sowing as fresh as possible in autumn/fall. Cut up tubers when dormant. H9

Gynandiris (Iridaceae)
Winter-dormant corms. Sow seed in spring. Separate when corms are dormant. H9

Gypsophila (Caryophyllaceae)
Perennials of varying sizes and habits. Sow seed in spring. Take stem cuttings of non-flowering growth in summer. H8

Haastia (Compositae)
Rosette-forming perennial making carpets or cushions. Sow fertile in spring, although autumn/fall sown seed when exposed to winter cold germinates better. Carefully detach newly formed rosettes at the end of summer and treat as cuttings. Overhead watering of cuttings is undesirable. H8

Habenaria see *Gymnadenia*

Haberlea (Gesneriaceae)
Rosette-forming perennials. Sow seed on chopped sphagnum moss in spring. Established clumps can be divided in spring. Make cuttings of newly formed mature leaves. H8

Habranthus (Amaryllidaceae)
Winter-dormant bulbs. Sow seed in spring. Separate bulbs whilst dormant. Bulb cuttage; twin scaling. H8–9

Hackelia (Boraginaceae)
Perennial. Sow seed in spring. H8

Hacquetia epipactis (Umbelliferae)
Perennial. Sow seed in spring. Divide established clumps as they start into growth. H8

Haemodorum (Haemodoraceae)
Difficult perennials. Sow seed in spring. H9

Halenia (Gentianaceae)
Annuals, biennials and short-lived perennials. Sow seed in spring. H7–8

× *Halimocistus* (Cistaceae)
Small evergreen shrubs. Bigeneric hybrids between species of *Cistus* and *Halimum*. Take stem cuttings of non-flowering growth in late summer. H8–9

Halimum (Cistaceae)
Small evergreen shrubs of varying sizes. Sow seed in spring. Take stem cuttings in late summer. H8–9

Haplocarpha (Compositae)
Difficult perennials. Sow fertile seed in spring. H9–10

Haplopappus (Compositae)
Perennials, sometimes short-lived and small shrubs of varying sizes. Sow fertile seed in spring. Take stem cuttings of new growth in late spring or early summer. H8–9

Hardenbergia (Leguminosae)
Evergreen sprawlers or climbers. Spring sow seed after soaking for 24 hours in boiling water. Take stem cuttings of non-flowering growth in autumn/fall. H9–10

Harrimanella stelleriana (Ericaceae)
Evergreen sub-shrub. Sow seed in spring on chopped sphagnum moss. Take stem cuttings in autumn/fall; cuttings can be slow to root. H7

Hastingsia see *Schoenolirion*

Haylockia (Amaryllidaceae)
Summer-dormant bulbs of varying sizes. Sow seed in spring. Separate bulbs when dormant; twin scaling. H9

125

Hebe (Scrophulariaceae)
A large genus of evergreen shrubs of varying sizes and habits. As species in cultivation tend to hybridise, seed should be collected only from isolated plants. Sow seed in spring. Take stem cuttings of non-flowering growth in autumn/fall. H8–9

Hebenstretia (Selaginaceae)
Evergreen shrubs and perennials of varying sizes. Sow seed in spring. Take stem cuttings of non-flowering growth in summer. H9

Hectorella caespitosa (Hectorellaceae)
Cushion-forming sub-shrub, difficult in cultivation. Sow fertile seed as fresh as possible; cold seems to stimulate germination. Detach newly formed mature rosettes and treat as cuttings; avoid overhead watering. H8

Hedera (Araliaceae)
Evergreen woody climbers. The juvenile forms are climbing and the smallest-leaved cultivars may be used to cover rocks. Adult forms, which are much branched, make small slow-growing shrubs. Stem cuttings or leaf bud cuttings taken in late summer are easy to root, but stem cuttings of adult forms also taken in late summer are slow and difficult. H7–9

Hedysarum (Leguminosae)
Annuals, perennials and evergreen shrubs. Sow seed in spring after soaking for 24 hours in cold water. Division is sometimes possible of clump-forming species if there is not a single tap root. Take stem cuttings in autumn/fall. H8–9

Helianthemum (Cistaceae)
Prostrate evergreen sub-shrubs. Sow seed in spring. Take stem cuttings of new growth in summer. H8–9

Helichrysum (Compositae)
Perennials, often short-lived and evergreen shrubs, all of varying sizes and habits. Sow fertile seed in spring. Take stem cuttings of non-flowering growth of woody subjects in autumn/fall. Clump formers can be divided as they start into growth. Some of the shrubs which have scale-like leaves, e.g. *H. selago*, are better if leaves are not removed from cutting. H8–9

Heliophila (Cruciferae)
Annuals and perennials that can become woody with age. Sow seed in spring. Take stem cuttings of non-flowering growth in late summer. H8

Heliosperma (Caryophyllaceae)
Tufted perennials. Sow seed in spring. Divide clumps as they come into growth. Take summer stem cuttings of non-flowering growth. H8

Helipterum (Compositae)
Annuals and perennials that can be short lived. Sow seed in spring. Divide as plants come into growth. H8–9

Helleborus (Ranunculaceae)
Perennials, sometimes with woody stems. Sow seed immediately it is ripe and expose to winter cold. Old seed is difficult to germinate, erratic and can be long delayed. Soaking in cold water for 24 hours before sowing will sometimes help. Divide following flowering. H7–8

Helonias (Melanthiaceae)
Perennial. Sow seed in autumn/fall and expose to winter cold; germination can be erratic and delayed. Divide in spring as growth is about to start. H8

Heloniopsis (Melanthiaceae)
Perennial. Sow seed in autumn/fall and expose to winter cold; germination can be erratic and delayed. Divide as growth starts. Mature new leaves will sometimes root. H8

Helxine see *Soleirolia*

Hepatica (Ranunculaceae)
Perennial. Sow seed in autumn/fall as fresh as possible and expose to winter cold; old seed germinates erratically and can be delayed. Doubles and other cultivars can be divided following flowering. H8

Herbertia (Iridaceae)
Winter-dormant bulbs of varying sizes. Sow seed in spring. Separate when bulbs are dormant. H9

Hermodactylus tuberosa (Iridaceae)
Perennial. Sow seed in spring. Divide following flowering. H9

Herniaria (Caryophyllaceae)
Mat-forming perennials that can become woody with age. Sow seed in spring. Divide as plants come into growth. Take stem cuttings of non-flowering growth in autumn/fall. H8

Herpolirion novae-zelandae (Anthericaceae)
Tuberous perennial. Sow seed in spring. Divide following flowering. H8

Hesperanthera (Iridaceae)
Corms. Sow seed in spring. Separate corms when dormant. H9

127

Hesperocalli sundulata (Hyacinthaceae)
Bulb. Sow seed in spring. Separate bulbs when dormant. H10

Hesperochiron (Hydrophyllacea)
Perennials with succulent leaves. Sow seed in spring. H9

Heterocentron (Melastomaceae)
Perennials or sub-shrubs. Sow seed in spring. Take stem cuttings of non-flowering growth in late summer. H9–10

Heteropappus (Compositae)
Perennials. Sow seed in spring. Divide as plants start into growth. H8

Heterotheca see *Chrysopsis*

Heuchera (Saxifragaceae)
Perennials of varying sizes. Sow seed in spring. Divide as plants start into growth. H8–9

× *Heucherella* (*Heuchera* sp. × *Tiarella* sp.) (Saxifragaceae)
Perennials, perhaps a little big for a rock garden. Divide as plants come into growth. H8

Hewardia see *Isophysus*

Hibbertia (Dilleniaceae)
Shrubs and sub-shrubs of varying sizes, including climbers; only a few species suitable for a rock garden. Sow seed in spring. Take cuttings of non-flowering growth in autumn/fall. H8–10

Hieracium (Compositae)
A large genus of perennials of varying sizes and qualities; some are weeds. Sow seed in spring. Divide clumps when there are multiheads on a tap root, in spring. H8

Himantoglossum hircinum (Orchidaceae)
Terrestrial orchid. Divide following flowering. H8

Hippeastrum (Amaryllidaceae)
(Now contains species which were formerly in other genera.) Bulbs of varying sizes. Sow seed in spring. Separate bulbs when not in active growth; bulb cuttage, twin scaling. H8–10

Hippocrepis (Leguminosae)
Mat-forming perennials of varying qualities. Sow seed after soaking for 24 hours in cold water. Some species can be divided in spring as growth starts. Take stem cuttings in summer of non-flowering growth. H8

Hirpicium (Compositae)
Perennial. Sow fertile seed in spring. Take stem cuttings of non-flowering growth if possible in autumn/fall. H9

Homeria (Iridaceae)
Corms of varying sizes. Sow seed in spring. Separate when dormant. Some produce cormlets in leaf axils. H9–10

Homogyne (Compositae)
Perennial. Sow seed in spring. Divide clumps as they come into growth. H8

Horminium pyrenaicum (Labiat)
Perennial. Sow seed in spring. Divide clumps as they start into growth. H8

Hosta (Hostaceae)
Perennials of varying sizes with a few small enough for a rock garden. Sow seed in spring. Divide as plants start into growth. H7–8

Houstonia (Rubiaceae)
Annuals and perennials. Sow seed in spring. Divide as plants start into growth. H8

Houttuynia cordata (Saururaceae)
Fetid perennial for a moist soil; can become invasive. Sow seed in spring. Divide as plants start into growth. H8

Hovea (Leguminosae)
Evergreen shrubs of varying sizes. Sow seed in spring after soaking for 24 hours in boiling water. Take stem cuttings in autumn/fall of non-flowering growth if possible. H9–10

Hudsonia (Cistaceae)
Evergreen sub-shrubs. Sow seed in spring. Take stem cuttings of non-flowering growth in autumn/fall. H7–8.

Hulsea (Compositae)
Annuals, biennials and perennials of varying sizes. Sow seed in spring. Divide as plants start into growth. H8–9

Hulthemia (**rosa**) *persica* (Rosaceae)
Deciduous shrub. Sow seed in autumn/fall. Stem cuttings taken in late summer will root, but success is variable. H8

Humata (Davalliaceae)
Epiphytic ferns. Separate rhizomes or divide them whilst dormant. H9

Hunnemania fumariifolia (Papaveraceae)
Perennial that can become woody at the base. Sow seed in spring. H9

Hutchinsia (Cruciferae)
Perennials of varying qualities. Sow seed in spring. Divide as plants start into growth. H7

Hyacinthus (Hyacinthaceae)
(Most species formerly in this genus have been transferred to others, e.g. *Hyacinthella, Hyacinthoides* and *Brimeura*.) Summer-dormant bulbs. Sow seed in spring. Separate when not in active growth; bulb cuttage, twin scaling. H7–8

Hydrastis (Ranunculaceae)
Perennial. Seed sown in autumn/fall gives best germination. Divide as plants start into growth. H8

Hydrocotyle (Umbelliferae)
Prostrate perennials that can be short lived; of varying qualities and can be weedy. Sow seed in spring. Divide as plants start into growth. H8

Hylomecon japonicum (Papaveraceae)
Perennial. Sow seed in spring. Divide as plants start into growth. H8

Hymenanthera alpina (Violaceae)
Slow-growing evergreen shrub, perhaps small enough for a large rock garden. Sow seed extracted from its fruits in spring. Take stem cuttings in autumn/fall. H8

Hymenopappus (Compositae)
Perennials. Sow seed in spring. Take cuttings of non-flowering growth in autumn/fall. H8–9

Hymenophyllum (Hymenophyllaceae)
Filmy ferns, generally not easy. Separate as new growth is about to start. H9

Hymenoxys (Compositae)
Perennials that can be temperamental in cultivation. Sow fertile seed in spring. H8

Hypecoum (Fumariaceae)
Annuals. Sow seed in spring. H8

Hypericum (Hypericaceae)
Annuals, perennials and shrubs of varying sizes and qualities. Sow seed in spring. Take stem cuttings of non-flowering growth in late summer. H7–9

Hypochoeris (Compositae)
Perennials of varying qualities. Sow seed in spring. Divide as plants start into growth. H8

Hypodomatium (Aspleniaceae)
Rhizomatous ferns. Divide as plants start into growth. H8

Hypoxis (Hypoxidaceae)
Corms of varying qualities. Sow seed in spring. Separate corms when dormant. H9–10

Hypsela (Campanulaceae)
Perennials. Sow seed in spring. Divide as plants start into growth. H8

Hyssopus (Labiatae)
Aromatic evergreen sub-shrubs. Sow seed in spring. Take stem cuttings of non-flowering growth in summer. H8

Iberis (Cruciferae)
Perennials that can become woody with age. Sow seed in spring. Take stem cuttings in summer. H8

Ilex (Aquifoliaceae)
Evergreen and deciduous shrubs including trees of which one or two, e.g. *I. crenata*, are small enough for a rock garden. Autumn/fall sow seed after extracting from berries and expose to winter cold; germination can be delayed and erratic. Take stem cuttings of evergreens in winter, wound and root over bottom heat. H7–8

Impatiens (Balsamaceae)
Annuals and perennials of varying habits, heights and qualities; some are weeds. Whilst spring-sown seed is usual, there is short viability. Take stem cuttings of non-flowering growth, if possible, in autumn/fall. H8–10

Incarvillea (Bignoniaceae)
Perennials and sub-shrubs. Sow seed in spring. Take cuttings of woody species in autumn/fall. H8–9

Inula (Compositae)
Perennials of varying sizes and qualities. Sow seed in spring. Divide during winter. H7–8

Ionopsidium (Cruciferae)
Annuals sometimes used as fillers. Sow seed where they are to flower in early autumn/fall. H8

131

Ipheion (Alliaceae)
(*Beauverdia* sometimes included with this genus.) Summer-dormant bulbs; some, which are less hardy, come into growth in autumn/fall. In favourable conditions *I. uniflorum* can be invasive. Sow seed in spring. Separate bulbs when dormant. H8–9

Iphigenia (Colchicaceae)
Corms. Sow seed in spring. Separate corms when dormant. H9

Ipomopsis (Polemoniaceae)
Perennials, usually monocarpic. Sow seed in spring. H8

Isophysis (Iridaceae)
Difficult perennials. Sow seed in spring. Divide as plants start into growth. H8

Iris (Iridaceae)
Large genus of perennials that can be tufted, rhizomatous or bulbous. There is variation in size and many are too large for a rock garden. Sow seed in spring. Oncocyclus and Juno group have seeds which contain chemical inhibitors. Soak, for at least 24 hours before sowing, in plenty of cold water and change this once or twice. Tufted kinds can be divided as they start into growth. Bulbs of the Reticulata group can be separated when dormant. Rhizomatous kinds are divided after flowering. Juno Iris are divided when dormant, but care must be taken not to damage fleshy roots. Broken or cut pieces of fleshy roots of species within the Juno group will sometimes produce new bulbs. H7–9

Isopogon (Proteaceae)
Evergreen shrubs of varying sizes. Sow seed in spring; germination can be erratic and delayed. H9

Isopyrum (Ranunculaceae)
Perennial. Sow seed in autumn/fall and expose to winter cold; germination can be delayed. H8

Isotoma (Campanulaceae/Lobeliaceae)
Perennial carpeters. Sow seed in spring. Pull apart when not in active growth. H8–9

Ixia (Iridaceae)
Winter-dormant corms of varying sizes. Sow seed in spring. Separate corms whilst dormant. H9–10

Ixiolirion (Ixioliriaceae)
Winter-dormant bulbs, perhaps rather large for a rock garden. Sow seed in spring. Separate bulbs when dormant. H9

Ixodia (Compositae)
Small evergreen shrubs. Sow fertile seed in spring. Take stem cuttings in late summer of non-flowering growth. H9

Jaborosa integrifolia (Solanaceae)
Creeping underground perennial; can be invasive. Sow seed in spring. Divide when not in active growth. H8

Jacobinia (Acanthaceae)
Perennials or small shrubs. Sow seed in spring. Take stem cuttings in autumn/fall of non-flowering growth, if possible. H9–10

Jankaea heldreichii (Gesneriaceae)
Rosette-forming perennial. Sow seed on chopped sphagnum moss in spring. Divide established clumps, if strong-willed, as plants start into growth. Take off new fully mature leaves and treat as cuttings. H8

× *Jankaemonda* (*Jankaea heldreichii* × *Ramonda pyrenaica*) (Gesneriaceae)
Perennial. Divide established clumps. Take off new fully mature leaves as cuttings. H8

Jasione (Campanulaceae)
Biennial or short-lived perennials. Sow fertile seed in spring. Divide established clumps as they start into growth. H8

Jasminum parkeri (Oleaceae)
Small evergreen shrub. Sow seed after extraction from fruit in spring. Take stem cuttings of non-flowering growth in late summer. H8

Jeffersonia (Berberidaceae/Podophyllaceae)
Perennials. Sow seed immediately it is ripe for best germination; spring-sown seed is less reliable. Divide as plants die back after flowering. H7

Jepsonia (Saxifragaceae)
Tuberous perennial. Sow seed in spring. Divide tubers as they start into growth. H8–9

Jovellana (Scrophulariaceae)
Evergreen sub-shrubs or perennials. Sow seed in spring. Take stem cuttings of non-flowering growth in autumn/fall. H9

Jovibarba (Crassulaceae)
Succulent rosette-forming perennials. Sow seed in spring. Detach offsets in late summer. H9

133

Juniperus (Cupressaceae)
Evergreen coniferous trees and shrubs of varying sizes and habits and with small cultivars of many species. Sow seed of species in autumn/fall. Take stem cuttings in winter with better results after frost; wound cuttings and root over bottom heat. H6–9

Jurinea (Compositae)
Perennials of varying sizes and qualities. Sow seed in spring. Division in spring as plants start into growth is sometimes possible. H8

Kalmia (Ericaceae)
Evergreen shrubs of varying sizes. Sow seed in spring on chopped sphagnum moss. Take stem cuttings in autumn/fall; success can be variable. Low growing shoots can be layered in late summer. H7–8

Kalmiopsis leachiana (Ericaceae)
Small evergreen shrub. Sow seed in spring on chopped sphagnum moss. Take stem cuttings of non-flowering new growth in late summer. H7–8

Kelseya uniflora (Rosaceae)
Evergreen sub-shrub forming flat cushions, difficult in cultivation. Sow fertile seed in autumn/fall and expose to winter cold. Individual rosettes taken from the circumference of cushions and treated as cuttings will sometimes root. H8

Kennedya (Leguminosae)
Sprawlers or woody climbers of varying sizes. Sow seed in spring after soaking in boiling water for 24 hours. Take stem cuttings of non-flowering growth if possible, in autumn/fall. H8–10

Kleinia (Compositae)
Usually succulent perennials or shrubs of varying sizes. Sow seed in spring. Take stem cuttings of non-flowering growth in autumn/fall. H9–10

Knautia (Dipsacaceae)
Perennials of varying qualities. Sow seed in spring. Divide established clumps as they start into growth. H7–8

Kohlrauschia (Caryophyllaceae)
Annuals, sometimes perennials, often short lived and of little merit. Sow seed in spring. H7

Korolkowii see *Fritillaria*

Kunzea (Myrtaceae)
Evergreen shrubs of varying sizes. Sow seed in spring. Take stem cuttings in late summer. H9–10

Lachenalia (Hyacinthaceae)
Summer-dormant bulbs. Sow seed in spring. Separate bulbs when not in active growth. Make cuttings of newly developed leaves; success variable. Twin scaling. H9–10

Lactuca (Compositae)
Annuals and perennials of varying sizes and habits. Sow fertile seed in spring. H7

Lagenifera see *Lagenophora*

Lagenophora (Compositae)
Perennials. Sow fertile seed in spring. Take stem cuttings in autumn/fall. Divide as plants start into growth. H9

Lagotis (Scrophulariaceae)
Perennials that are often difficult. Sow seed in spring. Division in early spring is sometimes possible. H7–8

Lamium (Labiateae)
Perennials of varying sizes and qualities. Sow seed in spring. Take stem cuttings of new growth following flowering. H7–9

Lantana (Verbenaceae)
A large genus of evergreen shrubs of varying sizes, habits and qualities, some of which can be serious weeds. Sow seed in spring. Take stem cuttings of non-flowering growth in spring. H9–10

Lapeirousia (Iridaceae)
Winter-dormant corms often treated as annuals. Sow seed in spring. Separate corms when dormant. H8

Lapiedra (Amaryllidaceae)
Summer-dormant bulb. Sow seed in spring. Separate bulbs when dormant. H9

Lathraea (Scrophulariaceae)
Parasitic perennials on roots of various trees, but especially species of *Corylus populus* and *Salix*. Seed can be sown in spring, or immediately following collecting, around host trees. Sow thinly in pots in spring and following germination plant out at the base of intended hosts. Pieces of *Lathraea* planted at the base of hosts will sometimes establish. H8

Lathyrus (Leguminosae)
Annuals and perennials of varying sizes, habits and qualities. Sow seed in spring after soaking seed for 24 hours in cold water. Divide in early spring. H7–8

Laurentia (Campanulaceae)
Prostrate perennials, often short lived. Sow seed in spring. Divide when not in active growth. H9

Lavandula (Labiatae)
Aromatic evergreen shrubs of varying sizes with small cultivars. Sow seed in spring. Take stem cuttings of non-flowering growth in late summer. H8–9

Lechenaultia (Goodeniaceae)
Beautiful annuals, perennial and shrubs that are difficult to keep. Sow fresh and fertile seed in spring. H9

Ledebouria see *Scilla*

Ledum (Ericaceae)
Aromatic evergreen shrubs of varying habits and sizes. Sow seed on chopped sphagnum moss in spring. Take stem cuttings in autumn/fall. H6

Leiophyllum buxifolium (Ericaceae)
Evergreen shrub, variable in size and habit. Sow seed in spring on chopped sphagnum moss. Take stem cuttings of non-flowering growth in autumn/fall. Prostrate forms can be layered in late summer. H8

Leontice (Berberidaceae/Leonticaceae)
Summer-dormant tubers. Sow seed in spring, although there is better germination if sown immediately it is ripe. Cut up tuber when dormant. H8–9

Leontopodium (Compositae)
Perennial. Sow seeds in spring. Take stem cuttings of non-flowering growth in summer. H6–8

Leopoldia see *Muscari*

Lepidium (Cruciferae)
Annuals, biennials and short-lived perennials, most of which are weedy. Sow seed in spring. H7

Lepidothamnus (Podocarpaceae)
Prostrate conifer. Sow seed in spring. Take stem cuttings in late autumn/fall, wound and root over bottom heat. H8

Lepisorus laxifolius (Polypodiaceae)
Fern. Divide when not in active growth. H8

Leptarrhena pyrifolia (*L. amplexifolia*) (Saxifragaceae)
Rhizomatous perennial. Sow seed in spring. Divide in early spring. H8

Leptinella (*Coptula*) (Compositae)
Perennial. Sow fertile seed in spring. H8

Leptospermum (Myrtaceae)
Evergreen shrubs of varying sizes and habits, of which only one or two species are suited to a rock garden. There are some small cultivars of *L. scoparium*. Sow seed in spring. Take stem cuttings of new growth in late summer. H8–9

Leptorhynchos (Compositae)
Perennials. Sow seed in spring. H8–9

Leschenaultia see *Lechenauttia*

Lespedeza (Leguminosae)
Evergreen or deciduous shrubs of widely varying sizes that in cold climates die back to ground level in winter. Sow seed in spring after soaking in cold water for 24 hours. H8–9

Lesquerella (Cruciferae)
Annuals and perennials often short lived. Sow seed in spring. H8–9

Leucanthemella (Compositae)
Perennial. Sow seed in spring. H8

Leucanthemopsis (Compositae)
Perennials, often short lived. Sow seed in spring. H8–9

Leucanthemum (Compositae)
Annuals and perennials. Sow seed in spring. Divide as plants start into growth. Take stem cuttings of non-flowering growth in summer. H8

Leuceria (Compositae)
Rosette-forming perennials, not easy in cultivation. Sow fertile seed in spring. H8–9

Leucocoryne (Alliaceae)
Summer-dormant bulbs. Sow seed in spring. Separate bulbs when dormant. H9

Leucocrinum montanum (Anthericaceae)
Tuberous perennial. Sow seed in spring. Divide following flowering. H9

Leucogenes (Compositae)
Perennial mat formers. Sow fertile seed in spring. Detach fully formed new rosettes and treat as cuttings. H8

Leucojum (Amaryllidaceae)
Summer-dormant bulbs. Sow seed in spring. Separate bulbs when dormant. Twin scaling. H8–9

Leucophyta see *Calocephalus*

Leucopogon (Epacridaceae)
Evergreen shrubs of varying sizes and habits; can be difficult to cultivate. Sow fresh seed in spring; germination can be difficult and erratic. Semi-mature stem cuttings taken in late summer will sometimes root. H9

Leucothoe (Ericaceae)
Evergreen shrubs of varying sizes. Sow seed in spring on chopped sphagnum moss. Take stem cuttings of non-flowering growth in autumn/fall. H8

Leuzea (*Centaurea*) (Compositae)
Biennials or short-lived perennials. Sow seed in spring. H8–9

Lewisia (Portulacaceae)
Perennials. Whilst spring sowing is more usual, there is better germination when seed is sown directly it has been gathered. Detach offsets from rosette-forming species in late summer and treat as cuttings. Divide herbaceous species in early spring before new growth starts. H7–9

Liabum (Compositae)
Rosette-forming perennials. Sow fertile seed in spring. H8–9

Libertia (Iridaceae)
Perennials of varying sizes and qualities. Sow seed in spring. Divide established clumps as new growth begins. H8–9

Lignocarpa (Umbelliferae)
Perennials, usually dioecious. Sow fertile seed in spring. H8

Lilium (Liliaceae)
Winter-dormant bulbs of varying sizes, only a few are small enough for a rock garden. Most of these have immediate germination and so can be sown in spring. Separate bulbs and take off bulblets when dormant. Take off outer scales of dormant bulbs. H8–9

Limnanthes (Limnanthaceae)
Annuals often used as fillers; better when sown in autumn/fall for spring flowering. H8

Limonium (Plumbaginaceae)
Annuals or perennials of varying sizes and qualities. Sow seed in spring. Divide as plants start into growth. Take root cuttings in late autumn/fall; success variable. H7–8

Linanthus see *Gilia*

Linaria (Scrophulariaceae)
Annuals and perennials of varying sizes and qualities. Sow seed in spring. Divide as plants start into growth. H7–9

Lindelofia (Boraginaceae)
Perennials of varying sizes and qualities. Sow seed in spring. Divide following flowering. Take root cuttings in autumn/fall. H8

Lindsaea (Dennstaedtiaceae)
Ferns. Divide as they start into growth. H8–9

Linnaea borealis (Primulaceae)
Prostrate evergreen sub-shrub that in general is not easy in cultivation. Sow seed in spring. Take stem cuttings in late summer. Divide as plants start into growth. H7

Linum (Linaceae)
Annuals, perennials and sub-shrubs. Sow seed in spring. Clump-forming perennials can be divided in spring or alternatively take soft stem cuttings in late spring and root under mist or in a closed case; stem cuttings of shrubby species are better taken in late summer. H8–9

Liparis (Orchidaceae)
Terrestrial orchids. Divide following flowering. H8

Lippia (Verbenaceae)
Perennials and evergreen or deciduous shrubs of varying sizes and qualities of which only one or two species are suited to a rock garden, and in favourable conditions these can be invasive. Sow seed in spring. Divide as plants come into growth in spring. H8–9

Liriope (Convallariaceae)
Perennial. Sow seed extracted from fruit in spring. Divide as plants start into growth. H8

Lissanthe (Epacidridaceae)
Small evergreen shrubs that can be prostrate. Sow fresh seed in spring. Germination, which is not easy, can be erratic and delayed. Success with late summer stem cuttings is variable. H8–9

Listera (Orchidaceae)
Terrestrial orchids. Divide following flowering. H8

Lithodora see *Lithospermum*

Lithophragma (Saxifragaceae)
Summer-dormant tubers. Sow seed in spring. Separate following flowering.
H7–8

Lithospermum (Boraginaceae)
Evergreen perennials or sub-shrubs. Sow seed in spring. Take soft stem
cuttings of non-flowering growth in late spring or early summer. H8

Lloydia serotina (Liliaceae)
Bulb. Sow seed in spring. Separate bulbs when dormant. H6–7

Loasa (Loasaceae)
Perennials or sub-shrubs usually treated as annuals. Plants with showy flowers
have stinging hairs. Sow seed in spring. H10

Lobelia (Campanulaceae/Lobeliaceae)
A large genus that includes annuals, perennials, aquatics, shrubs and even
trees. The giant species from the African mountains, although true alpines, are
too large for a rock garden and need special facilities for cultivation. Sow seed
in spring. Divide perennial species in spring. H8–9

Lobularia see *Alyssum*

Loiseleuria procumbens (Ericaceae)
Prostrate evergreen shrub that is difficult in cultivation. Sow seed on chopped
sphagnum moss in spring. Divide in early spring. Take stem cuttings of new,
non-flowering growth in summer. H6

Lomaria see *Blechnum*

Lomatium (Umbelliferae)
Difficult perennials. Sow seed in spring. H7–8

Lotus (Leguminosae)
Perennials and sub-shrubs of varying sizes and habits. Sow seed in spring after
soaking for 24 hours in cold water. Take cuttings of non-flowering growth in
summer. H7–9

Loxogramme (Grammitidaceae)
Rhizomatous ferns. Divide as plants start into growth. H8–9

Luetkia pectinatus (Rosaceae)
Evergreen suckering shrub. Sow seed in autumn/fall and expose to winter cold. Detach and pot suckers when not in active growth. Take stem cuttings of new growth in early summer. H7–8

Luina (Compositae)
Perennials of varying qualities. Sow seed in spring. Divide as plants start into growth. H8

Lupinus (Leguminosae)
Annuals, perennials and shrubs of varying sizes. Sow seed in spring. Divide perennials as they come into growth. Stem cuttings are sometimes available; take in early summer. H7–9

Luzuriaga (Philesiaceae)
Perennials, the stems of which can become woody with age. Sow seed in spring. Divide as plants start into growth. H8–9

Lyallia see *Hectorella*

Lychnis (Caryophyllaceae)
Perennials of varying sizes, habits and qualities. Sow seed in spring. Divide in early spring. H7–8

Lycopodium (Lycopodiaceae)
Perennial fern ally. Divide as plants start into growth. H6–8

Lycoris (Amaryllidaceae)
Summer-dormant bulbs; rather large for a rock garden. Sow seed in spring. Separate bulbs when dormant. Bulb cuttage; twin scaling. H9

Lygodium (Schizaceae)
Climbing ferns. Divide as plants start into growth. H9

Lysimachia (Primulaceae)
Biennials and perennials of varying sizes and qualities. Sow seed in spring. Divide in early spring. H7–8

Lysionotus (Gesneriaceae)
Evergreen sub-shrubs. Sow seed on chopped sphagnum moss. Take stem cuttings of non-flowering growth in late summer. H9

Maianthemum (Convallariaceae)
Perennials. Sow seed in autumn/fall and expose to winter cold. Germination can be delayed. Divide established clumps as they start into growth. H6–7

Malope (Malvaceae)
Annuals and short-lived perennials. Sow seed in spring. H8

Malva (Malvaceae)
Annuals and perennials that can be short lived; of varying sizes, habits and qualities. Sow seed in spring. Take stem cuttings of non-flowering growth when possible in late summer. H8

Malvastrum (Malvaceae)
Perennials of varying sizes and habits. Sow seed in spring. Take stem cuttings of non-flowering growth in late summer. H8–9

Mandragora (Solanaceae)
Tuberous perennials. Sow seed in spring. H9

Margyricarpus setosus (Rosaceae)
Evergreen shrub. Although seed can be spring sown, it germinates better if exposed to winter cold. Take stem cuttings of non-flowering growth in late summer. H8

Marrubium (Labiateae)
Aromatic perennials, some of which are rather coarse. Sow seed in spring. Take stem cuttings of non-flowering growth in autumn/fall. H8

Massonia (Hyacinthaceae)
Summer-dormant bulbs. Sow seed in spring. Separate bulbs whilst dormant. Twin scaling. H9

Mastigostyla (Iridaceae)
Bulbs. Sow seed in spring. Separate bulbs when dormant. H9

Matthiola (Cruciferae)
Perennials or sub-shrubs. Sow seed in spring. Take stem cuttings of non-flowering growth in late summer. H9

Mazus (Scrophulariaceae)
Prostrate perennials. Sow seed in spring. Divide as growth begins. Take stem cuttings in summer. H8

Meconopsis (Papaveraceae)
Biennials, monocarpic and perennials of varying sizes. Sow seed in spring although seed sown in autumn/fall quickly germinates to provide plantlets to overwinter. Divide perennial species as plants start into growth in spring. H7–8

142

Mecardonia (Scrophulariaceae)
Perennials grown for their fruit. Sow seed in spring. H9–10

Medeola virginica (Convallariaceae)
Perennial. Sow seed in autumn/fall and expose to winter cold; germination can be delayed. Divide after flowering. H7

Meehania (Labiatae)
Perennial. Sow seed in spring. Divide as plants start into growth. H8

Melandrium see *Lychnis*

Melasphaerula ramosa (*M. graminea*) (Iridaceae)
Summer-dormant corm. Sow seed in spring. Separate corms whilst dormant. H9

Mellitis melissophyllum (Labiatae)
Perennial. Sow seed in spring. Divide as plants start into growth. H8

Mentha requienii (Labiatae)
Aromatic perennial. Sow seed in spring. Divide as plants start into growth. H8

Menziesia (Ericaceae)
Evergreen shrubs of varying sizes. Sow seed in spring on chopped sphagnum moss. Take stem cuttings of maturing new growth produced after flowering. Young bushes can sometimes be divided in early spring before new growth starts. H7–8

Merendera (Colchicaceae)
Summer-dormant corms. Sow seed in spring. Separate corms when dormant. H8

Mertensia (Boraginaceae)
Perennials that can be difficult to keep. Sow seed in spring. Divide as plants start into growth. H8

Micranthus (Iridaceae)
Corm. Sow seed in spring. Separate corms whilst dormant. H9–10

Microcachrys tetragona (Podocarpaceae)
Prostrate evergreen conifer. Sow seed in spring. Take stem cuttings in winter, wound and root over bottom heat. H8

Microlepia (Dennstaediaceae)
Rhizomatous ferns. Divide as they start into growth. H8–9

143

Micromeria (Labiatae)
Aromatic perennials or sub-shrubs. Sow seed in spring. Take stem cuttings of non-flowering growth in summer. H8–9

Micromyrtus (Myrtaceae)
Small or prostrate evergreen shrubs. Sow seed in spring. Take cuttings of non-flowering growth in autumn/fall. H9

Milla (Alliaceae)
Corm. Sow seed in spring. Separate corms when dormant. H8

Milligania (Asteliaceae)
Tufted perennial. Sow seed in spring. Divide established clumps as they pass out of flower. H8

Mimosa (Leguminosae)
Evergreen shrubs of varying sizes. *M. pudica* and *M. sensitiva* sometimes grown as annuals for their sensitive, folding leaves. Spring sow seed after soaking for 24 hours in boiling water. H10

Mimulus (Scrophulariaceae)
A large genus including annuals, perennials and small shrubs of varying habits. Sow seed in spring. Divide clump-formers as they come into growth. Take stem cuttings of both perennial and shrubby species in autumn/fall. H7–10

Minuartia (Caryophyllaceae)
A large genus containing annuals and perennials of varying habits and qualities. Sow seed in spring. Divide as plants start into growth. Take stem cuttings of non-flowering growth in summer. H8

Mitchella (Rubiaceae)
Trailing woody evergreens. Sow seed in spring, although cold stimulates germination. Take stem cuttings of new growth in late spring and root under mist or in a closed case. H7–8

Mitella (Saxifragaceae)
Perennial. Sow seed in spring. Divide as plants start into growth. H7–8

Mitraria coccinea (Gesneriaceae)
Evergreen prostrate or scandent shrub. Sow seed in spring on chopped sphagnum moss. Take stem cuttings of non-flowering growth in autumn/fall. H9

Mitrasacme (Loganiaceae)
Perennials of varying habits including carpets and loose cushions. Sow seed in spring. Divide as plants start into growth. H8–9

Moehringia (Caryophyllaceae)
Annuals and perennials of varying qualities. Sow seed in spring. Divide as plants start into growth. H8

Moltkia (Boraginaceae)
Perennials, becoming woody with age, or sub-shrubs. Sow seed in spring. Take stem cuttings of non-flowering growth in autumn/fall. H8

Monardella (Labiatae)
Low-growing or prostrate perennials, becoming woody with age. Sow seed in spring. Take stem cuttings of non-flowering growth in late spring or early summer. H8–9

Moneses uniflora (Pyrolaceae)
Difficult small perennial. Sow autumn/fall seed as soon as it is ripe on chopped sphagnum; germination is difficult and at the best, erratic. Divide in spring; results variable. H7–8

Monsonia (Geraniaceae)
Perennials, becoming woody with age, or sub-shrubs. Sow seed in spring. Take stem cuttings, of non-flowering growth if possible, in autumn/fall. H9–10

Montia (Portulacaceae)
Annuals or perennials of varying qualities. Sow seed in spring. Divide when not in active growth. H8

Moraea (Iridaceae)
Rhizomatous or corms of varying sizes. Sow seed in spring. Separate corms or divide when dormant. H9

Morisia monanthos (*M. hypogaea*) (Cruciferae)
Perennial. Sow seed in spring. Take root cuttings in autumn/fall. H8

Muehlenbeckia (Polygonaceae)
Deciduous and evergreen shrubs, often climbing; a few creeping or prostrate species, which can be invasive, suited to a rock garden. Sow seed in spring. Take stem cuttings of young growth in late spring. Young plants can be divided in early spring; success variable. H8

Muendenia see *Aceriphyllum*

Muilla (Alliaceae)
Corms. Sow seed in spring. Separate corms when dormant. H8–9

145

Muscari (Hyacinthaceae)
Summer-dormant bulbs that in favourable conditions can be invasive. Sow seed in spring. Separate bulbs when dormant. Twin-scaling. H7–8

Muscarimia see *Muscari*

Myosotidium hortensia (Boraginaceae)
Perennial suited only to large rock gardens. Whilst seed can be spring sown, there is a short viability and it is preferable to sow as soon as collected. H8

Myosotis (Boraginaceae)
Annuals and perennials often short lived. Sow seed in spring. Divide after flowering. H7–8

Myrsine nummularia (Myrsinaceae)
Low-growing to prostrate evergreen shrub, usually dioecious. Sow seed after extracting from fruit in spring. Take cuttings of non-fruiting growth in autumn/fall. H8–9

Myrteola nummularia (Myrtaceae)
Prostrate evergreen shrub. Sow seed in spring. Take stem cuttings of non-fruiting growth in autumn/fall. H8

Nama (Hydrophyllaceae)
Annuals and perennials that can become woody with age. Sow seed in spring. H9

Nandina domestica (Berberidaceae)
Evergreen shrub; whilst the species is too large for a rock garden, there are many small cultivars. Divide when not in active growth. Take stem cuttings in late summer. H8–9

Narcissus (Amaryllidaceae)
Summer-dormant bulbs. Sow seed in spring or sow as soon as it is ripe. Detach and separate bulbs whilst dormant. Twin-scaling. H7–9

Nardophyllum (Compositae)
Small evergreen shrubs. Sow fertile seed in spring. Take stem cuttings of non-flowering growth in late summer. H8

Narthecium (Melanthiaceae)
Perennial. Sow seed in spring, although winter cold will stimulate germination. Divide established clumps at the end of winter. H6–7

Nassauvia (Compositae)
Difficult perennials. Sow fertile seed in spring. Rosettes detached when fully mature in late summer can be treated as cuttings. H8

Nastanthus see *Acarpha*

Nemastylis (Iridaceae)
Bulb. Sow seed in spring. Separate bulbs when dormant. H9

Neomarica (Iridaceae)
Rhizomatous perennials. Rather large for a rock garden. Sow seed in spring. Divide in early spring. H9–10

Nepeta (Labiatae)
Perennials of varying sizes and habits. Sow seed in spring. Take stem cuttings of non-flowering growth in summer or autumn/fall. Divide as plants start into growth. H8

Nephrolepis (Davalliaceae)
Ferns of varying sizes. Divide as plants start into growth. Some species and their forms can be increased by leaf cuttings. H9–10

Nerine (Amaryllidaceae)
Summer-dormant bulbs of varying sizes. Sow seed in spring. Separate bulbs when dormant. Bulb cuttage; twin-scaling. H8–10

Nertera (Rubiaceae)
Perennial carpeters grown for fruit. Sow seed in spring. Divide as plants start into growth. H8–9

Nierembergia (Solanaceae)
Perennials. Sow seed in spring. Take non-flowering stem cuttings in summer; cutting back some shoots about four weeks before taking cuttings increases propagating material. Creeping species are divided as plants start into growth. H8–9

Nigritella nigra (Orchidaceae)
Terrestrial orchid. Divide following flowering. H8

Nivenia (Iridaceae)
Perennials that can become woody with age. Sow seed in spring. Detach fans with some stem in spring and treat as cuttings. H9

Nolana (Nolanaceae)
Showy annuals that can be used as fillers. Sow seed in spring. H10

Nomocharis (Liliaceae)
Winter-dormant bulbs that are a challenge to grow. Sow seed in spring. Separate bulbs when dormant; detach outer scales when lifting. H7–8

Notholaena (Polypodiaceae)
Mostly desert ferns, going dormant at the onset of summer in nature although in cultivation they can be kept growing by watering. Divide as plants start into growth. H9

Notholirion (Liliaceae)
Bulbs. Sow seed in spring. Separate bulbs when dormant. H8–9

Nothoscordium (Alliaceae)
Bulbs. *N. inodorum* is a noxious weed. Sow seed in spring. Separate bulbs when dormant. H8

Notothlaspi (Cruciferae)
Difficult rosette-forming monocarpic perennials. Sow seed in spring. Germination difficult; cold often stimulates germination. H8

Nototriche (Malvaceae)
Difficult perennials, many forming cushions. Sow fertile seed in spring. H8

Oaksiella see *Uvularia*

Odontospermum see *Asteriscus*

Odontostomum hartwegii (Tecophilaeaceae)
Winter-dormant corm. Sow seed in spring. Separate corms when dormant. H9

Oenothera (Onagraceae)
A large genus of perennials of varying sizes and qualities. Sow seed in spring. Those with multiple crowns can be divided in early spring. Take root cuttings of those with thick roots in autumn/fall. H7–9

Olearia (Compositae)
A large genus of evergreen shrubs of varying sizes, of which a few species or small cultivars would have a place on a rock garden. Sow fertile seed in spring. Take stem cuttings of maturing growth in autumn/fall. H8–9

Omphalodes (Boraginaceae)
Perennials. Sow seed in spring. Divide following flowering. H8

Omphalogramma (Primulaceae)
Perennials. Sow seed, which can have short viability, in spring. Divide following flowering. H7–8

Onixotis (Dipidax)

Onobrychis (Leguminosae)
Annuals, perennials and small evergreen shrubs that can be difficult. Sow seed in spring after soaking in cold water for 24 hours. Take stem cuttings where possible of non-flowering growth in autumn/fall. H8–9

Onoclea sensibilis (Aspleniaceae)
Stoloniferous fern. Divide when dormant. H8

Ononis (Leguminosae)
Annuals, perennials and small evergreen shrubs. Sow seed in spring after soaking for 24 hours in cold water. Divide perennials as plants start into growth. Take stem cuttings of non-flowering growth of shrubs in autumn/fall. H8–9

Onosma (Boraginaceae)
A large genus of annuals and perennials, which can be short lived, and sub-shrubs of varying qualities. Sow seed in spring. Take stem cuttings of maturing new growth produced after flowering. H8

Onychium (Adiantaceae)
Ferns. Divide as plants start into growth. H8–9

Ophioglossum (Ophioglossaceae)
Ferns with separate fertile fronds, not all of which are easy to cultivate. Divide when dormant. H8–9

Ophiopogon (Convallariaceae)
Sow seed in spring after extracting from fruit. *O. planiscapus* 'Nigrescens' comes true from seed as long as seedlings are rogued. Divide established clumps in spring. H8–9

Ophrys (Orchidaceae)
Summer-dormant terrestrial orchids. Divide immediately following flowering. H8–9

Opithandra (Gesneriaceae)
Evergreen perennials. Sow seed in spring on chopped sphagnum moss. Divide established clumps in early spring. Take off mature new leaves as cuttings. H9

Orchis (Orchidaceae)
Many species formerly in this genus now appear in others. Divide as plants pass out of flower. H8

Oreobolos (Cyperaceae)
Perennials forming mats or cushions, often short lived. Sow fertile seed in spring on chopped sphagnum moss. Detach rooted portions in spring. As mats or cushions begin to fall apart, pull to pieces. H8

Oreocharis (Gesneriaceae)
Rosette-forming perennials. Sow seed on chopped sphagnum moss in spring. Divide established clumps in early spring. Detach fully mature new leaves and make into cuttings. H9

149

Oreophylax see *Gentiana*

Oreopolus see *Cruckshankia*

Oreorchis (Orchidaceae)
Terrestrial orchids. Divide following flowering. H8

Oreostylidium subulatum (Stylidiaceae)
Stoloniferous, tufted perennial. Sow seed in spring. Detach offsets in late summer. H8

Oresitrophe (Saxifragaceae)
Perennials. Sow seed in spring, although exposure to cold seems to stimulate germination. Divide as plants start into growth. H8

Origanum (Labiatae)
Aromatic perennials that can become woody with age; of varying habits and vigour. Sow seed in spring. Take stem cuttings of non-flowering growth in late summer. Divide established clumps as they start into growth. H8–9

Orites (Proteaceae)
Difficult small evergreen shrubs. Sow seed in spring after soaking for 24 hours in cold water. Germination can be delayed and difficult. H8–9

Ornithogalum (Hyacinthaceae)
Summer-dormant bulbs of varying sizes and qualities. Sow seed in spring. Separate bulbs when dormant. Twin scaling. H8–9

Ornithopus (Leguminosae)
Annuals and perennials of varying qualities. Sow seed after soaking for 24 hours in cold water in spring. H8–9

Orobus see *Lathyrus*

Orostachys (Crassulaceae)
Perennials with succulent monocarpic rosettes. Sow seed in spring. Detach offsets and if without roots, treat as cuttings. H9

Orphanidesia gaultherioides (Ericaceae)
Evergreen sub-shrub, usually prostrate. Sow seed in spring on chopped sphagnum moss. Take cuttings of new growth as it matures in late summer. Its prostrate habit permits layering in late summer. H8

Orphium frutescens (Gentianaceae)
Small evergreen shrub. Sow seed in spring. Take stem cuttings of non-flowering growth in autumn/fall. H9

Orthrosanthos (Iridaceae)
Perennials. Sow seed in spring. Detach fans with roots if possible, if not treat as cuttings. H9

Orychophragmus (Cruciferae)
Perennial. Sow seed in spring. H9–10

Osteospermum (Compositae)
Perennials of varying sizes and habits. Sow seed in spring. Take stem cuttings, of non-flowering growth if possible, in autumn/fall. H8–9

Otanthus maritimus (Compositae)
Perennial that can be short lived. Sow seed in spring. Divide as plants start into growth. Take stem cuttings of non-flowering growth in summer. H9

Othonna (Compositae)
Perennials, often tuberous and evergreen shrubs. Sow seed in spring. Divide perennials in early spring. Take stem cuttings in summer. H9

Othonnopsis see *Othonna*

Ourisia (Scrophulariaceae)
Perennials. Sow fertile seed in spring. Divide as plants start into growth. Take stem cuttings in late summer. H8

Oxalis (Oxalidaceae)
A large genus of perennials, many of which are tuberous and some become woody; of varying qualities, some are noxious weeds. Sow seed in spring. Separate tubers when dormant; sometimes there can be tubercles in the leaf axils. Divide non-tuberous forms when not in active growth. H7–9

Oxycoccus see *Vaccinium*

Oxygraphis (Ranunculaceae)
Perennials that are difficult to keep. Sow seed in autumn/fall and exposed to winter cold; germination can be difficult and delayed. H6–7

Oxylobium (Leguminosae)
Evergreen shrubs of varying sizes and habits. Sow seed in spring after soaking for 24 hours in boiling water. Take stem cuttings of non-flowering growth in autumn/fall. H9–10

Oxytropis (Leguminosae)
Perennials or sub-shrubs. Sow seed in spring after soaking for 24 hours in cold water. Take stem cuttings of shrubby species in autumn/fall. H8

Pachyphytum (Crassulaceae)
Rosette-forming succulent perennials. Sow seed in spring. Detach offsets in autumn/fall. H9–10

Pachysandra (Buxaceae)
Self-sterile perennials that can become woody with age. Sow seed after extracting from fruit in spring. Take stem cuttings in autumn/fall. Divide after flowering. H8

Pachystegia minor (Compositae)
Small evergreen shrub. Sow fertile seed in spring. Take stem cuttings in autumn/fall. H8

Pachystima see *Paxistima*

Paeonia (Paeoniaceae)
Perennials and shrubs of varying sizes and habits, most of which are too large for a rock garden. Sow fully developed seeds before or as seed pods open and expose to winter cold, with germination usually occurring in the following spring. Older seed should be autumn/fall sown with exposure to winter cold; germination can be erratic and long delayed. Herbaceous kinds can be lifted when dormant and the fleshy roots cut into pieces, each with a terminal bud. Woody *P. potaninii*, which has a suckering habit, can be divided in early spring. H8

Pancratium (Amaryllidaceae).
Winter-dormant bulbs. Sow seed in spring. Separate bulbs when dormant; bulb cuttage; twin scaling. H8–9

Papaver (Papaveraceae)
Annuals and perennials of varying sizes. Sow seed in spring. Divide as plants start into growth. Root cuttings of species with thicker roots prepared in late autumn/fall will often produce new plants. H7–8

Paradesia see *Anthericum*

Parahebe (Scrophulariaceae)
Perennials and small shrubs. Sow seed in spring. Divide clump-forming perennials in spring. Take stem cuttings of non-flowering growth in autumn/fall. H8–9

Paraquilegia (Ranunculaceae)
Self-sterile perennials. Sow seed in spring or in autumn/fall and expose to winter cold. Divide following flowering. H8

152

Parathelypteris (Thelypteridaceae)
Rhizomatous ferns of varying sizes. Divide when dormant. H9–10

Paris (Trilliaceae)
Rather difficult rhizomatous perennials. Sow seed in autumn/fall and expose to winter cold. Old seed germinates erratically and can be long delayed. H8

Parnassia (Saxifragaceae)
Perennials. Best germination from autumn/fall sown seed when exposed to winter cold. Divide plants as they start into growth. H7–8

Parochetus communis (Leguminosae)
Perennial, sometimes tuberous. Sow seed in spring after soaking for 24 hours in cold water. Divide as plants come into growth. H7–9

Paronychia (Caryophyllaceae)
Annuals or perennials, often mat forming. Sow seed in spring. Divide as plants start into growth. Take stem cuttings in autumn/fall. H8

Parrya (Cruciferae)
Perennial. Sow seed in spring; germination can be erratic. H8

Pasithea coerulea (Anthericaceae)
Rhizomatous perennial. Sow seed in spring. Divide as plants start into growth. H9

Patersonia (Iridaceae)
Perennials. Sow seed in spring. Divide established clumps ensuring each fan has roots. H9–10

Patrinia (Valerianaceae)
Perennials of varying sizes. Sow seed in spring. Divide as plants start into growth. H8

Pedicularis (Scrophulariaceae)
Showy semi-parasitic perennials, almost impossible to cultivate. Sow seeds thinly and introduce amongst host plants; success variable. H8

Pelargonium (Geraniaceae)
Large genus including shrubs and perennials some of which are tuberous; variable in size and habit. Sow seed in spring. Some of the perennials can be divided in spring. Cut up the tubers when dormant. Take stem cuttings of non-flowering growth if possible in autumn/fall. H8–10

153

Pellaea (Synoperidiaceae)
Ferns of varying sizes. Divide whilst dormant. H8–10

Penstemon (Scrophulariaceae)
A large genus of perennials with some shrubs. Sow seed in spring. Take semi-mature stem cuttings in summer. H8–10

Pentachondra (Epacridaceae)
Low-growing or prostrate evergreen shrubs; often dioecious. Sow seed in spring on chopped sphagnum moss; germination can be difficult. Take stem cuttings in late summer of maturing growth; success variable. H8

Pentapera sicula see *Erica*

Perezia (Compositae)
Annuals and perennials. Sow fertile seed in spring. Take soft cuttings in late spring. H8

Pernettya (Ericaceae)
Small evergreen shrubs grown for their fruits. Sow seed extracted from fruits in spring. Young clumps can be divided in spring. Take stem cuttings in autumn/fall. H8

Petrocallis (Cruciferae)
Mat or cushion forming perennials. Sow seed in spring. Detach new rosettes in late summer and treat as cuttings. H8

Petrocoptis (Caryophyllaceae)
Perennials of tufted habit. Sow seed in spring. Divide as plants start into growth. Take stem cuttings in summer of non-flowering growth. H9

Petrocosmea (Gesneriaceae)
Perennials. Sow seed in spring on chopped sphagnum moss. Divide established clumps as they start into growth. Take fully mature new leaves and make into cuttings. H8–9

Petromarulea pinnata (Campanulaceae)
Rosette-forming perennial. Sow seed in spring. H9

Petrophytum (Rosaceae)
Mound-forming tufted perennials. Sow seed in autumn/fall and expose to winter cold. Take off rooted pieces in spring as growth begins. Detach rosettes in late summer and treat as cuttings. H7–8

Petrorhagia (Caryophyllaceae)
Annuals and perennials of varying qualities. Sow seed in spring. Divide as plants come into growth. Take stem cuttings in spring. H7–8

Phacelia (Hydrophyllaceae)
Annuals or perennials that can be short lived. Sow seed in spring. H8

Phegopteris (Thelypteridiaceae)
Ferns of varying sizes. Divide whilst dormant. H8

× *Philageria veitchii* (*Philesia magellanica* × *Lapageria rosea*) (Philesiaceae)
Creeping or sprawling sub-shrub. Divide when well established. H8

Philesia magellanica (Philesiaceae)
Evergreen sub-shrub, slow to establish but then runs around. Sow fertile seed in spring when available. Take off newly formed rooted plants in early spring. H8

Phlomis (Labiatae)
Perennials or evergreen shrubs of varying habits and sizes. Sow seed in spring. Divide well-established clumps of perennials. Take stem cuttings of new mature growth in summer. H8–9

Phlox (Polemoniaceae)
Perennials of varying habits and sizes. Sow seed in spring. Take stem cuttings of non-flowering growth in summer. Some, perhaps all, can be increased by root cuttings taken in late autumn/fall. Divide as plants start into growth or following flowering. H7–8

Phormium tenax 'Alpina Purpurea (Phormiaceae)
Divide as plants start into growth. H8

Phuyopsis stylosa (Valerianceae)
Perennial. Sow seed in spring. Divide as plants start into growth. Take stem cuttings of non-flowering growth in autumn/fall. H7–8

Phyla see *Lippia*

Phylica (Rhamnaceae)
Evergreen shrubs of varying sizes. Sow seed in spring. Take stem cuttings of new growth in late summer. H9–10

Phyllachne (Stylidiaceae)
Cushion-forming sub-shrubs, not easy. Sow fertile seed in spring on chopped sphagnum moss. Take off newly formed rosettes at the end of summer and treat as cuttings. H8

155

Phyllactis (Valerianiaceae)
Difficult perennial of varying habits, mostly rosette-forming. Sow seed in spring. H8

Phyllitis (Aspleniaceae)
Hart's tongue fern. Divide as plants start into growth. H8

× *Phylliopsis hillieri* (*Phyllodoce breweri* × *Kalmiopsis leachiana*) (Ericaceae)
Evergreen small shrub. Take stem cuttings in autumn/fall. H7

Phyllodoce (Ericaceae)
Small evergreen shrubs. Sow seed in spring on chopped sphagnum moss. Take stem cuttings in late summer or early autumn/fall; it is better not to remove scale-like leaves. H6–8

× *Phyllothamnus erectus* (*Phyllodoce empetriformis* × *Rhodothamnus chamaecistus*) (Ericaceae)
Small evergreen shrub. Take stem cuttings of new growth in autumn/fall. H8

Physaria (Cruciferae)
Perennials. Sow seed in spring. H9

Physoplexis comosus (*Phyteuma cohosum*) (Campanulaceae)
Perennials, of which some forms seem to be self-sterile. Sow fertile seed as fresh as possible in spring. Take root cuttings in late autumn/fall. H8

Phyteuma (Campanulacea)
Annuals and short-lived perennials. Sow seed in spring. H8

Picea (Pinaceae)
Evergreen coniferous trees, of which many species have produced small cultivars. Stem cuttings of new growth taken in winter, wounded and inserted in a rooting medium over bottom heat will sometimes root. Success is variable and sometimes atypical plants result. Side graft in late winter onto seedling stock of the same species is possible. H6–8

Pieris nana see *Arcterica nana*

Pimelea (Thymelaecaeae)
Evergreen shrubs of varying sizes. Sow seed in spring. Take cuttings of non-flowering growth in autumn/fall. H8–9

Pinellia (Araceae)
Tuberous perennial. Although spring sowing of seed is usual, there is better germination if sown in late summer as soon as it is ripe. Cut up tubers whilst dormant. H8–9

156

Pinguicula (Lentibulariaceae)
Rosette-forming insectivorous plants. Sow seed in spring on chopped sphagnum moss. Divide well-established clumps in early spring. Take off fully mature new leaves as cuttings. H7–9

Pinus (Pinaceae)
Evergreen coniferous shrubs and trees. Even the smallest species is too large for a rock garden, but many species have produced small cultivars. Stem cuttings of new growth taken in winter, wounded and inserted over bottom heat will sometimes root, but resulting plants may be atypical. Side graft onto seedling stock of the same species if possible. H6–9

Pityrogramma (Hemionitidaceae)
Ferns of varying sizes. Divide whilst dormant. H8–10

Placea (Amaryllidaceae)
Bulbs. Sow seed in spring. Separate bulbs when dormant. Bulb cuttage; twin scaling. H9

Plagiorrhegma see *Jeffersonia*

Plantago (Plantaginaceae)
Annuals and perennials, some of which can become woody with age; they are of varying qualities and some are weeds. Sow seed in spring. H7–9

Platanthera (Orchidaceae)
Terrestrial orchids. Divide as plants finish flowering. H8

Platycodon grandiflorum var. *apoyama* (Campanulaceae)
This dwarf form hybridises with the straight species, which can reach 3ft (1m), and so seedlings lose their dwarfness. In a garden collect seed only from plants grown in isolation. Sow seed in spring. H8

Playtcrater arguta (Hydrangeaceae)
Small deciduous shrub, often prostrate. Sow seed in spring. Take stem cuttings in late summer. H8

Pleione (Orchidaceae)
Epiphytic orchids. Separate newly formed pseudobulbs whilst dormant. Sometimes tiny pseudobulbs develop on the tip of new plump ones. H9

Pleopeltis (Polypodiaceae)
Ferns of varying sizes. Divide whilst dormant. H8

Podocarpus (Podocarpaceae/Taxaceae)
Evergreen conifers, mostly trees but one or two species are small enough for a rock garden. Sow seed in spring. Take stem cuttings in winter and insert over bottom heat after wounding. H7–8

Podolepis (Compositae)
Perennials. Sow fertile seed in spring. Separate rosettes in spring. H8–9

Podophyllum (Podophyllaceae)
Perennials. Sow seed in spring after removing from fruit and washing. Divide established clumps as they start into growth. H7–8

Pogonia (Orchidaceae)
Terrestrial orchids. Divide following flowering. H8

Polemonium (Polemoniaceae)
Perennials of varying sizes. Sow seed in spring. Divide as plants start into growth. H7–8

Polianthes tuberosa (Agavaceae)
Tuberous perennial. Sow seed in spring. Divide whilst dormant. H9

Polygala (Polygalaceae)
A large genus including annuals, perennials and shrubs of varying sizes and qualities. Sow seed in spring. Divide perennials as they start into growth. Take stem cuttings in autumn/fall. H7–9

Polygonatum (Convallariaceae)
Rhizomatous perennials of varying sizes. Sow seed in autumn/fall and expose to winter cold; germination can be delayed. Divide as plants start into growth. H6–8

Polygonum (Polygonaceae)
Perennials of varying habits, sizes and qualities. Sow seed in spring. Take stem cuttings of non-flowering growth in autumn/fall. Divide as plants start into growth. H6–8

Polypodium (Polypodiaceae)
Many species formerly in the genus have been transferred to others. Ferns of varying sizes. Divide when not in active growth. H8

Polystichum (Dryopteridiaceae/Aspleniaceae)
Ferns of varying sizes. Divide when dormant. H8

Polyxena (Hyacinthaceae)
Bulbs. Sow seed in spring. Separate bulbs when dormant. H8–9

Portulaca (Portulacaceae)
Annuals and perennials, often short lived. Sow seed in spring. H8–9

Potentilla (Rosaceae)
Perennials of varying sizes and qualities; one small deciduous shrub, *P. fruticosa*, which has many forms and cultivars. Sow seed in autumn/fall and expose to winter cold. Divide in spring. Take stem cuttings from *P. fruticosa* of non-flowering growth in summer. H7–8

Poterium see *Sanguisorba*

Prasophyllum (Orchidaceae)
Terrestrial orchids. Divide following flowering. H9

Pratia (Campanulaceae)
Creeping perennials. Sow seed in spring. Take cuttings of non-fruiting growth, if possible, in late summer. H8

Primula (Primulaceae)
A large genus of perennials of varying habits. Whilst seed is usually spring sown, some gardeners prefer to sow some species, e.g. candelebra group, immediately seed has been collected to produce seedlings to overwinter. All species with multiple crowns can be divided: spring bloomers after flowering; summer and later bloomers as they start into growth. *P. palinuri* and *P. forrestii* and some other species produce woody stems with rosettes attached; these can be taken off and treated as cuttings. On occasions, plantlets may appear amongst inflorescence; these should be detached and treated as cuttings. *P. denticulata* and its cultivars can be increased by root cuttings taken from mid to late summer. *P. wollastonii* and *P. kisoana* produce runners or stolons with plantlets at their ends. Some, perhaps all, species within the petiolarid group can be increased by leaf cuttings. H7–9

Prionotes cerinthoides (Epacridaceae)
Epiphytic evergreen woody sprawler or climber that is not easy. Sow fertile seed on chopped sphagnum moss in spring. Success with stem cuttings is variable; but best results have been from those prepared from soft new growth in late spring. It is sometimes possible to divide as plants start into growth. H9

Prostanthera (Labiatae)
Aromatic evergreen shrubs of varying sizes. Sow seed in spring. Take stem cuttings in autumn/fall. H8–10

Prunella (Labiatae)
Perennials of varying qualities. Sow seed in spring. Divide when not in active growth. H7–8

Prunus (Rosaceae)
Evergreen and deciduous trees and shrubs of varying sizes and habits, of which at least *P. prostrata*, *P. pumila* and *P. tenella* and its forms could have a place on

a rock garden. Moist stored seed of species should be autumn/fall sown, after extracting from their fruit, and exposed to winter cold. Stem cuttings taken from soft growth in late spring or early summer and inserted under mist or in a closed case will root, but success is variable. Layering can be carried out in late summer. H7–8

Pseudocytisus see *Vella*

Pseudomuscari see *Muscari*

Pseudotsuga (Pinaceae)
Evergreen coniferous trees of which some species have produced small cultivars. Stem cuttings taken in winter, wounded and inserted over bottom heat will sometimes root. Side graft at the end of winter onto seedlings of *P. taxifolia*. H8

Psoralea (Leguminosae)
Perennials, sometimes short lived, and shrubs of varying sizes and qualities. Sow seed in spring after soaking for 24 hours in cold water. Take stem cuttings of shrubs in late summer or autumn/fall of non-flowering growth. H9

Pteridophyllum racemosa (Papaveraceae/Pteridophyllaceae)
Perennial. Sow seed as fresh as possible and expose to winter cold. Division after flowering gives variable results. H7

Pteris (Pteridaceae/Adiantaceae/Dennstaedtiaceae)
Ferns of varying sizes. Divide when not in active growth. H9–10

Pterocephalus (Dipsacaceae)
Perennial. Sow fertile seed in spring. Divide plants as they start into growth. Take stem cuttings of new growth in late spring. H8

Pterostylis (Orchidaceae)
Terrestrial orchids. Divide following flowering. H8–9

Pterygopappus lawrencei (Compositae)
Evergreen sub-shrub making a hard cushion. Sow fertile seed in spring. Take off newly formed rosettes from the edge of cushion and treat as cuttings. H8

Ptilotrichum see *Alyssum*

Ptilotus (Amaranthaceae)
A large genus of annuals and perennials that can be short lived. Sow fertile seed in spring. Take stem cuttings in late spring or early summer; suitable material

can be difficult to find. Cutting hard back may sacrifice flowers but it will increase cutting material. H9–10

Pulmonaria (Boraginacae)
Perennial of varying sizes and qualities; when plants are happy they can self sow to such an extent that they can become a nuisance. Sow seed in spring. Divide following flowering. H7

Pulsatilla (Ranunculacae)
Perennials. For best results sow seed as soon as it has been collected. Germination success declines with age of seed until it can be erratic and long delayed. Prepare root cuttings as soon as plants become dormant in summer. H7

Pultenaea (Leguminosae)
Evergreen shrubs of varying sizes. Sow seed in spring after soaking for 24 hours in boiling water. Stem cuttings taken in late summer of non-flowering growth may root, but success is variable. H9

Punica granatum **'Nana'** (Punicaceae)
Small deciduous shrub. Sow seed in spring. Take stem cuttings of non-flowering growth in summer. H9

Pushkinia scilloides (Hyacinthaceae)
Summer-dormant bulb. Sow seed in spring. Separate bulbs when dormant. H7

Putoria (Rubiaceae)
Low-growing evergreen shrubs. Sow seed in spring. Take stem cuttings of soft growth in spring. H8–9

Pycnophyllum (Caryophyllaceae)
Perennials forming mats or cushions. Sow seed in spring. H9

Pygmaea see *Chionohebe*

Pyrola (Pyrolaceae)
Difficult perennials. Sow seed immediately it is ripe on chopped sphagnum moss and expose to winter cold; germination difficult. Divide well-established clumps as they start into growth; success variable. H7

Pyrolirion see *Zephyranthes*

Pyrrosia (Polypodiaceae)
Small ferns. Divide as plants start into growth. H8

Pyxidanthera barbulata (Diapensiaceae)
Difficult, creeping evergreen shrub. Sow fresh seed on chopped sphagnum moss and expose to winter cold; old seed is difficult and erratic in germination. Take stem cuttings of maturing growth in late summer. H8

Raffenalda (Cruciferae)
Perennials. Sow seed in spring; germination can be delayed. Root cuttings taken in late summer are sometimes successful. H8

Ramonda (Gesneriaceae)
Rosette-forming perennials. Sow seed in spring on chopped sphagnum moss. Divide established clumps in spring. Take off fully mature new leaves and make into cuttings. H7–8

Ranunculus (Ranunculaceae)
A very large genus of perennials of varying sizes, habits and qualities; some can be weeds. Sow seed when mature, even if it is green, and expose to winter cold; germination ought to occur in the following spring. Germination of old seed can be long delayed. Southern hemisphere species rarely germinate in under two years; Germination of Australasian species can be speeded up by storing seed packets in a refrigerator for four weeks. No seed container should be discarded in under three years. A few species produce runners. Some, e.g. *R. ficaria* and *R. asiaticus*, have root tubers and can be divided; retain a portion of stem with each propagule as they start into growth. H6–9

Ranzania japonica (Berberidaceae)
Perennials. Sow seed as soon as it is ripe and expose to winter cold. Divide as growth starts. H8

Raoulia (Compositae)
Evergreen sub-shrubs that fall into two groups: the easy carpeting scabweeds and the difficult cushion vegetable sheep; there are hybrids between species of both groups. Sow fertile seed in spring. Scabweeds, which often root as they grow, can be pulled apart at the end of winter. When natural rooting does not occur, detach fully mature rosettes at the end of summer and treat as cuttings or cut out tufts of growth and treat these as cuttings. From the vegetable sheep, carefully detach new fully formed rosettes and treat as cuttings; avoid overhead watering. H7–8

Reineckia carnea (Convallariaceae)
Perennial carpeter. Sow seed in autumn/fall after removal from fruit; cold stimulates germination, which can be erratic and delayed. Pull apart established clumps before they start into growth. The variegated form is unstable and propagules should be only of the best striped leaves. H8

162

Relbunium (Rubiaceae)
Short-lived perennial carpeter grown for its fruits. Sow seed on chopped sphagnum moss in spring. Pull apart in spring as new growth commences. H10

Restio (Restoniaceae)
Dioecious handsome grass-like perennials. Sow fertile seed, which has short viability, in spring; germination is erratic. Old plants resent disturbance. Divide young plants as growth is about to start in spring; success is variable. H8–10

Rhabdothamnus solandri (Gesneriaceae)
Slow-growing evergreen shrub. Sow seed in spring. Take stem cuttings of non-flowering growth in late summer. H9

Rhamnus (Rhamnaceae)
Deciduous and evergreen shrubs of varying habits and sizes that are sometimes dioecious; only one or two are suited to a rock garden. Sow seed in autumn/fall and expose to winter cold; germination can be erratic and delayed. Take stem cuttings in late summer. H7–8

Rhazya orientalis (Apolcynaceae)
Perennial. Sow seed in spring. Divide as plants start into growth. H8

Rheum (Polygonaceae)
Perennials of varying sizes and qualities. Seed often fails to germinate because it has short viability which is further reduced by poor storage. It is preferable to sow as soon as it is ripe and expose to winter cold for best germination, although if seed is fresh it can be spring sown. H7–8

Rhinopetalum see *Fritillaria*

Rhodiola (Crassulaceae)
Perennials with succulent leaves. Sow seed in spring. Divide at the end of winter. Take stem cuttings in late summer of, if possible, non-flowering growth. H7

Rhododendron (Ericaceae)
Deciduous and evergreen shrubs of varying sizes and habits. The smaller and the prostrate species would have a place on the rock or peat garden. Sow seed in spring on chopped sphagnum moss. Take stem cuttings of maturing new growth during the summer. Deciduous species are more difficult to root successfully from cuttings. Take stem cuttings from soft new growth in spring; insert into rooting medium in a deep pot or tray/flat and cover with a sheet of glass or polythene; water from below. Do not disturb until it can be seen that rooting has taken place. Encourage secondary growth before or immediately

after potting, otherwise survival over winter can be poor. Layering is usually possible and is best if carried out at the end of winter. Grafting is undesirable and should be practised only if all other forms of propagation fail. Make a side graft in late winter onto stock of a seedling species from the same series. H7–9

Rhodohypoxis (Hypoxidaceae)
Winter-dormant tubers. Sow seed in spring; progeny variable. Separate tubers when dormant. H8–9

Rhodophiala see Hippeastrum

Rhodothamnus chamaecistus (Ericaceae)
Small evergreen shrub. Sow seed in spring on chopped sphagnum moss. Take stem cuttings of maturing new growth in late summer. H8

Rhoea see Tradescantia

Richea (Epacridaceae)
Evergreen shrubs of varying sizes, but most are small enough for a rock garden; none are easy to cultivate. Seed, which has a short viability, should be sown immediately it is ripe on chopped sphagnum moss; germination difficult. Stem cuttings of growth taken in late summer may root, but success is variable. H8–9

Ricotia (Cruciferae)
Perennials, the stems of which can become woody with age. Sow seed in spring. H8

Rigidella (Iridaceae)
Winter-dormant bulbs. Sow seed in spring. Separate bulbs when dormant. H9

Rohdea japonica (Convallariaceae)
Rhizomatous perennial of which the Japanese have introduced many forms. Spring sow seed; germination can be delayed. Divide in early spring. H9

Romanzoffia (Hydrophyllaceae)
Perennials, sometimes rhizomatous. Sow seed in spring. Divide as plants start into growth. R. californica often produces tubercles in leaf axils. H8

Romulea (Iridaceae)
Corms. Sow seed in spring. Separate corms when not in active growth. H8–9

Rosa (Rosaceae)
A large genus of thorny deciduous and evergreen shrubs, including climbers; only a few species are suitable for growing on a rock garden. There are small cultivars of larger roses and a race of miniatures. Species can be raised from

seed extracted from their fruits, autumn/fall sown and exposed to winter cold; germination can be erratic and delayed. Some of the smaller species with a suckering habit, e.g. *R. pimpinellifolium*, can be lifted in winter and pulled apart. Most of the horticultural groups of roses can be rooted from cuttings with varying degrees of success. Best results are usually from summer stem cuttings, but often better still from leaf bud cuttings. Side or cleft grafting or T-budding should be practised on *R. canina*, *R. rugosa* or *B. laxa* only when other forms of propagation prove to be unsuccessful. Stem cuttings taken from miniatures will root at most times of the year, although there is best success when using non-flowering material. H7–9

Roscoea (Zingiberaceae)
Rhizomatous perennials. Sow seed in spring. Divide as plants start into growth. H8

Rosmarinus officinalis '**Prostratus**' and *R. lavandulaceus* (Labiatae)
Low-growing or prostrate aromatic evergreen shrubs. Take stem cuttings of non-flowering growth, when possible, in late summer. H8–9

Rossularia (Crassulariaceae)
Succulent rosette-forming perennials. Sow seed in spring. Detach offsets or rosettes and if without roots treat as cuttings. H8–9

Rubus (Rosaceae)
A large genus of deciduous and evergreen shrubs, many of which are climbing and spiny; a number are invasive and can be serious weeds. Sow seed in autumn/fall after extracting from fruit and expose to winter cold. Many kinds will layer if the tips of shoots in mid summer are brought to the ground and weighed down with stones. Creeping species and those which form clumps can be divided as they start into growth in spring. Stem cuttings or leaf-bud cuttings taken in summer will root. H7–8

Rupicapnos (Fumariaceae)
Short-lived perennials. Sow seed in spring. H8

Ruscus (Ruscaceae)
Dioecious evergreen (leafless) shrubs with creeping rootstocks. Seed extracted from fruit is better moist stored for spring sowing. Divide at the end of winter. H8–9

Ruta (Rutaceae)
Perennials, sometimes monocarpic or shrubs with fetid leaves. Sow seed in spring. Take stem cuttings of non-flowering growth in late summer. Apart from *R. graveolens* success can be variable. H8–9

Rydbergia see *Hymenoxys*

Sagina (Caryophyllaceae)
Perennials of varying habits and qualities. Sow seed in spring. Divide when not in active growth. H8

Salix (Salicaceae)
Deciduous dioecious trees and shrubs of varying sizes, habits and qualities. Take stem cuttings in winter after leaves have been shed. H6

Salvia (Labiatae)
A large genus which includes annuals, biennials, perennials and shrubs of varying sizes and habits. Sow seed in spring. Divide perennials as they start into growth. Take stem cuttings of non-flowering growth in autumn/fall. H7–10

Samolus (Primulaceae)
Annuals and perennials that may become woody at the base. Sow seed in spring. Divide as plants start into growth. H8

Sanguinaria canadensis (Papaveraceae)
Rhizomatous perennial. Sow seed in autumn/fall and expose to winter cold; germination can be delayed. Divide following flowering. H6

Sanguisorba (Rosaceae)
Perennials of varying sizes and qualities. Sow seed in autumn/fall and expose to winter cold; germination can be erratic. Divide as plants start into growth. H7

Santolina (Compositae)
Aromatic evergreen shrubs that are rather large for a rock garden. An exception is *S. elegans*, and some cultivars of *S. chamaecyparissus* are also small enough. Sow fertile seed of species in spring. Take stem cuttings in late summer. H8–9

Saponaria (Caryophyllaceae)
Annuals and perennials of varying sizes, habits and qualities. Sow seed in spring. Take stem cuttings in late summer. Some of the clump-formers can be divided as they start into growth. H8

Sarcocapnos (Fumariaceae)
Perennials, often short-lived. Sow seed in spring. H8–9

Sarcococca (Buxaceae)
Fragrant, small evergreen shrubs. Sow seed in spring. Take stem cuttings in autumn/fall. Divide following flowering. H8

Sarmienta repens (Gesneriaceae)
Creeping evergreen sub-shrub. Sow seed in spring on chopped sphagnum moss. Take stem cuttings of non-flowering growth in late summer. H9

Sarothamnus see *Cytisus*

Sarracenia (Sarraceniaceae)
Insectivorous perennials. Sow seed in spring on chopped sphagnum moss. Divide as plants start into growth. H9–10

Satureja (Labiatae)
Annuals, perennials and sub-shrubs with aromatic foliage. Sow seed in spring. Take stem cuttings of non-flowering growth in summer. Clump-formers can be divided as they start into growth. H8–9

Satyrium (Orchidaceae)
Terrestrial orchids. Divide immediately after flowering. H9–10

Saussurea (Compositae)
Perennials of varying sizes and qualities; whilst some can be weedy there are others which are difficult to cultivate. Sow fertile seed in spring. Division as plants start into growth is possible with some. H7

Saxifraga (Saxifragaceae)
Perennials of varying sizes, habits and qualities. This large genus includes annuals, biennials, monocarpic and perennial species. For convenience the genus has been divided into sections, the number and names of which vary according to classification; a few of these have little horticultural merit. Although plant habit within each section can be expected to be similar there are exceptions. There are some species which produce runners. e.g. *S. stolonifera* and *S. brunoniana*; new plantlets will be rooted by early autumn/fall. A few, e.g. *S. granulata*, produce tubercles amongst basal leaves or in the axils of stem leaves. Gather these before the aerial parts die away and store in moist peat or sand for spring planting. Clump-formers, e.g. *S. pennsylvanicum*, can be divided as they start into growth. Mossy saxifrages and other mat-formers can be lifted as they deteriorate and pulled apart with each rooted portion replanted. Stem cuttings can be taken of maturing new growth produced after flowering in late summer. There are many species within different sections that have broad rosettes, e.g. *S. paniculata*, *S. umbrosa* and *S. cotyledon*. Offsets can be detached as they mature after flowering and if without roots, treated as cuttings. In cushions (Porophyllum section), e.g. *S. burserana*, with many cultivars and hybrids, individual tight rosettes of mature new growth, produced after flowering, can be detached and treated as cuttings. Prostrate stem species such as *S. oppositifolia* are increased by stem cuttings of maturing new growth taken in summer. H6–9

Saxiglossum angustissimum (Polypodiaceae)
Creeping rhizomatous fern. Divide as plants start into growth. H8

Scabiosa (Dipsacaceae)
Annuals and perennials of varying sizes, habits and qualities. Sow fertile seed in spring. Take stem cuttings of non-flowering growth in autumn/fall. H8

Scaevola (Goodeniaceae)
Perennials and sub-shrubs of varying sizes and qualities. Sow seed in spring. Take stem cuttings of non-flowering growth in early autumn/fall. H8–9

Schivereckia (Cruciferae)
Perennials. Sow seed in spring. It is sometimes possible to divide established clumps as they go out of flower. H7

Schizocentron elegans (Melastomaceae)
Prostrate perennial. Sow seed in spring. Divide as plants start into growth. Take stem cuttings of non-flowering growth in late summer. H9–10

Schizocodon see *Shortia*

Schizostyllis (Iridaceae)
Perennials, perhaps a little large for a rock garden. Sow seed in spring. Divide as plants start into growth. H8

Schoenolirion (Hyacinthaceae)
Winter-dormant bulbs. Sow seed in spring. Separate bulbs when dormant. H9

Scilla (Hyacinthaceae)
(Species formerly in this genus may now be classified under *Hyacinthoides* or *Ledebouria*.) Bulbs of varying sizes and qualities. Sow seed in spring. Separate bulbs when dormant. Twin scaling. H7–9

Scleranthus (Caryophyllaceae)
Annuals and perennials of varying sizes, habits and qualities. Sow seed in spring. Divide clump-formers as they start into growth. Lift cushion-formers, if they deteriorate after new growth has been completed, and pull apart, replanting or potting rooted pieces. H8

Scoliopus (Trilliaceae)
Perennials. To ensure fertilisation on cultivated plants, transfer pollen with a camel-hair brush. Sow seed immediately it is ripe; although cold is not necessary for germination, it often stimulates it; there is poor and erratic germination with old seed. Divide established clumps after flowering. H8

Scorzonera (Compositae)
Perennials of varying sizes. Sow fertile seed in spring. Make root cuttings in autumn/fall. H8

Scutellaria (Labiatae)
Annuals, perennials and sub-shrubs of varying sizes, habits and qualities. Sow seed in spring. Take stem cuttings in summer. Divide clump-formers as they start into growth. H8

Sebaea (Gentianaceae)
Annuals and short-lived perennials; not easy in cultivation. Sow seed in spring. H8–9

Sedum (Crassulaceae)
A large genus of succulent perennials that also includes a few annuals. Sow seed in spring. Take stem cuttings of non-flowering growth of early bloomers in autumn/fall and late bloomers in late spring. When material is in short supply leaf-bud cuttings can be prepared in late summer. Evergreen species can be divided as plants start into growth. The herbaceous kinds can be divided at the same time when there is a multi-crown. Take off pieces of root with a growth bud, dip the cut surface into a fungicide and treat as cuttings until adventitious roots have been produced. H7–9

Selaginella (Selaginellaceae)
Perennial fern ally. Divide when not in active growth. H9–10

Selago (Globulariaceae/Selaginaceae)
Evergreen small shrubs. Sow seed in spring. Take stem cuttings of non-flowering growth in autumn/fall. H9

Selliera (Goodeniaceae)
Low-growing, even prostrate perennials. Sow seed in spring. Divide as plants start into growth. H8

Semiaquilegia (Ranunculaceae)
Perennials that can hybridise with *Aquilegia*. Although seed will germinate following spring sowing, there is more even and better germination when autumn/fall sown and exposed to winter cold. Divide established plants following flowering. H8

Sempervivella (Crassulaceae)
Rosette-forming succulent perennials. Sow seed in spring. Detach offsets after flowering. H8–9

169

Sempervivum (Crassulaceae)
Perennial succulents with monocarpic rosettes. Sow seed in spring. Detach offsets in late summer. H6–8

Senecio (Compositae)
A large genus including weedy ephemerals, annuals, perennials and shrubs of varying sizes, habits and qualities. Sow seed in spring. Clump-formers can be divided in late winter. Take stem cuttings of non-flowering growth in autumn/fall. H7–10

Serapias (Orchidaceae)
Terrestrial orchids. Divide following flowering. H8–9

Serissa foetida (Caprifoliaceae)
Small evergreen shrub. Sow seed in spring. Take stem cuttings of non-flowering growth in autumn/fall. H8

Serratula (Compositae)
Perennials varying in sizes and habits. Sow seed in spring. Divide as plants start into growth. H8–9

Shortia (Diapensiaceae)
Perennials forming loose rosettes; stems can become woody with age. Sow fertile seed on chopped sphagnum moss in autumn/fall and expose to winter cold for best germination. Seed sown in spring will usually germinate, although erratically, as long as seed is not old. Detach newly mature rosettes in late summer and treat as cuttings, unless they are already with roots. H7

Sibbaldia (Rosaceae)
Low-growing even prostrate perennials. Sow seed in autumn/fall and expose to winter cold. Divide as plants start into growth. Take stem cuttings in summer. H8

Sibthorpia (Scrophulariaceae)
Creeping perennials. Sow seed in spring. Take stem cuttings in spring or early summer. Plants root as they grow. H8

Sideritis (Labiatae)
Evergreen shrubs of varying sizes. Sow seed in spring. Take stem cuttings in late summer. H9

Sierversia see *Geum*

Silene (Caryophyllaceae)
Annuals and perennials of varying sizes, habits and qualities. Sow seed in spring. Divide as plants start into growth. Take stem cuttings of non-flowering growth in autumn/fall. H7–8

170

Simethis bicolor (Asphodelaceae)
Perennial. Sow seed in spring. Divide following flowering. H8

Sisyrinchium (Iridaceae)
Perennials of varying sizes and qualities. Sow seed in spring. Divide as plants start into growth, ensuring that each fan has some roots. H8–9

Smelowskia (Cruciferae)
Perennial, often short lived and not easy. Sow seed in spring. H7–8

Smilacina (Convallariaceae)
Perennials, most of which are too large for a rock garden. Sow seed in autumn/fall and expose to winter cold; germination can be delayed. Divide as plants start into growth. H6–7

Soldanella (Primulaceae)
Perennials. Whilst spring sowing is more usual, better results occur if sown immediately when ripe, and exposed to winter cold. Divide established clumps following flowering. H7

Soleirolia soleirolii (Urticaceae)
Perennial creeper. Unsuitable for the rock garden, for it can become a noxious weed. The golden or variegated leafed forms, which are less invasive, might be tolerated—but with caution. Take off rooted portion in spring. H8

Solenomelus see *Laurentia*

Solidago (Compositae)
Perennials of which only one or two are small enough for a rock garden. Sow seed in spring. Divide in late winter. H7

Sophora prostrata (Leguminosae)
Low-growing or prostrate evergreen shrub suited to a large rock garden. Sow seed in spring after soaking for 24 hours in boiling water. H8

Sorbus (Rosaceae)
Deciduous trees and shrubs of varying sizes of which *S. reducta*, *S. poteriifolia* and forms of *S. matsumurana* and *S. sambucifolia* might have a place on a rock garden. Sow seed after extraction from fruit in autumn/fall and expose to winter cold. There is a form of *S. reducta* that suckers, and this can be divided in spring. Soft cuttings taken in late spring or early summer and rooted under mist or in a closed case are sometimes successful. H6

Sparaxis (Iridaceae)
Winter-dormant corms, perhaps rather large for a rock garden. Sow seed in spring. Separate corms when not in active growth. H9

Speirantha gardenii (Convallariaceae)
Rhizomatous perennial. Sow seed in spring. Divide as plants start into growth. H8

Spenceria (Roseaceae)
Perennials. Sow seed in autumn/fall and expose to winter cold. Divide as plants start into growth. H8

Sphaeralcea (Malvaceae)
Perennials or sub-shrubs, most of which are rather large for a rock garden. Sow seed in spring. Take stem cuttings of new growth in early summer. H8–9

Sphenomeris (Dennstaedtiaceae)
Ferns that are not particularly easy. Divide as plants start into growth. H9

Spigelia (Loganiaceae)
Annuals and perennials of varying sizes. Sow seed in spring. Divide as plants start into growth. H8

Spiraea (Rosaceae)
Deciduous shrubs of varying sizes only a few of which are small enough for a rock garden. Sow seed in autumn/fall and expose to winter cold. Divide as plants start into growth. Take stem cuttings of non-flowering growth in summer. H7–8

Spiranthes (Orchidaceae)
Terrestrial orchids. Divide immediately following flowering. H8

Spraguea (Portulacaceae)
Perennials, often short lived. Sow seed in spring. H8

Sprekelia formosissima (Amaryllidaceae)
Bulb, rather large for a rock garden. Sow seed in spring. Take off bulblets when not in active growth. Bulb cuttage or twin scaling. H8–9

Sprengelia (Epacridaceae)
Mostly dioecious evergreen shrubs of varying sizes and habits. Sow seed as fresh as possible; germination can be difficult. Take stem cuttings of non-flowering new growth in autumn/fall; success variable. H8–9

Stachys (Labiatae)
Perennials of varying sizes; can be rather coarse. Sow seed in spring. Take stem cuttings of non-flowering growth in autumn/fall. Clumps can be divided in spring as growth begins. H8–9

Stackhousia (Stackhousiaceae)
Difficult perennials. Sow seed in spring. H8–9

Staehelina (Compositae)
Perennials that can become woody at the base, often short lived. Sow seed in spring. Take stem cuttings in summer. H8–9

Statice see *Limonium*

Stellera chamaejasme (Thymelaeaceae)
Perennial, choice but not easy to cultivate. Sow fertile seed on chopped sphagnum moss in spring; autumn/fall sowing with exposure to winter cold often gives better germination. H6–7

Stenandrium (Acanthaceae)
Perennials. Sow seed in spring. Divide established clumps in spring as plants start into growth. H9

Stenanthium (Melanthiaceae)
Winter-dormant bulbs. Sow seed in spring. Separate bulbs when dormant. H8

Stenomesson (Iridaceae)
Bulbs. Sow seed in spring. Separate bulbs when dormant. H9

Sternbergia (Amaryllidaceae)
Summer-dormant bulbs. Sow seed in spring. Divide bulbs when dormant. Twin scaling. H7–8

Stevia (Compositae)
Perennials that can be short lived. Sow seed in spring. H9

Stokesia laevis (Compositae)
Perennial, perhaps too large for a rock garden. Sow fertile seed in spring. Divide as plants start into growth. Take root cuttings in late autumn/fall. H8

Streptanthera (Iridaceae)
Corms. Sow seed in spring. Separate corms when dormant. H8–9

Streptocarpus (Gesneriaceae)
Of this large genus a few of the smaller species, whether caulescent or acaulescent, may have a place on a rock garden. Sow seed on chopped sphagnum moss in spring. Use fully mature new leaves to make cuttings of the acaulescent forms. Take stem cuttings of the caulescent forms in late summer. H9–10

173

Streptopus (Convallariaceae)
Perennials. Sow seed in autumn/fall and expose to winter cold; germination can be delayed. Divide following flowering. H6

Stylidium (Stylidiaceae)
Perennials, the flowers of which have sensitive styles, and which can be difficult to keep in cultivation. Sow seed in spring. Divide established clumps as they start into growth; success can be variable. H9

Stylophorum (Papaveraceae)
Perennials. Sow seed in spring. Divide as plants start into growth. H8

Stypandra (Phormiaceae)
Hummock-forming or low-growing perennials. Sow seed in spring. Divide as plants start into growth. H8–9

Styphelia (Epacidaceae)
Evergreen shrubs of varying sizes. Sow seed as fresh as possible; germination can be difficult. Take stem cuttings of non-flowering growth in autumn/fall; success variable. H9

Suttonia nummularia see **Myrsine numullaria**

Swainsona (Leguminosae)
Perennials and evergreen shrubs of varying sizes. Sow seed in spring after soaking for 24 hours in cold water. Take stem cuttings of non-flowering growth in late summer; success variable. H8–9

Swertia (Gentianaceae)
Annuals and perennials of varying sizes, sometimes short lived. Sow seed in spring. H8

Symphyandra (Campanulaceae)
Biennials and perennials that can be short lived. Sow seed in spring. Some can be divided as they start into growth. Take stem cuttings of young growth in early summer. H8

Symplocarpus foetida (Araceae)
Rather coarse perennial, needing a moist soil; its fetid flowers, which are produced in winter, are more curious than beautiful. Sow seed as it is ripe, with subsequent exposure to winter cold. Divide established clumps, taking off pieces of root with a growth bud after plants have flowered. H6–8

Synnotia (Iridaceae)
Corms. Sow seed in spring. Separate corms when dormant. H9

174

Synthyris (Scrophulariaceae)
Perennials that can be short lived. Sow seed in spring. Divide following flowering. H8

Syringodia (Iridaceae)
Corms. Sow seed in spring. Separate corms when dormant. H9–10

Talinum (Portulacaceae)
Perennials and sub-shrubs. Sow seed in spring. Divide clump-formers as they start into growth. Take stem cuttings in autumn/fall. H7–8

Tanacetum (Compositae)
Annuals and perennials that can become woody with age. Sow seed in spring. Divide as plants start into growth. Take stem cuttings in autumn/fall. H8

Tanakaea radicans (Saxifragaceae)
Dioecious perennial. Sow fertile seed in spring. Male plants produce runners and rooted plantlets can be taken in autumn/fall. Divide females as they start into growth. H8

Tapeinanthus see *Narcissus*

Taxus (Taxaceae)
Evergreen coniferous shrubs and trees. There are small cultivars that might have a place on a large rock garden. Take stem cuttings in winter and insert over bottom heat after wounding. H7–8

Tchihatchewia isatidea (Cruciferae)
Monocarpic perennial. Sow seed in spring. H8

Tecophilaea cyanocrocus (Tecophilaeaceae)
Winter-dormant corms. Sow seed in spring. Separate corms when dormant. H8

Teesdaliopsis (Cruciferae)
Rosette-forming perennial. Sow seed in spring. H7

Telesonix (Saxifragaceae)
Perennials. Sow seed in spring. Divide following flowering. H8

Tellima (Saxifragaceae)
Perennials. Sow seed in spring. Divide as plants start into growth. H8

Tetrademia see *Luina*

Tetratheca (Tremandraceae)
Perennials and sub-shrubs of varying habits and sizes that are not easy in cultivation. Sow seed in spring, but germination can be difficult. Take stem cuttings of non-flowering growth in autumn/fall. H9

Teucrium (Labiatae)
Perennials and evergreen shrubs of varying sizes. Sow seed in spring. Take stem cuttings of non-flowering growth in autumn/fall. Divide perennials as they start into growth. H8–9

Thalictrum (Ranunculaceae)
Perennials of varying sizes and qualities. Sow seed immediately collected in autumn/fall and expose to winter cold. Some species produce offsets; detach when rooted. Divide as plants start into growth. H7–8

Thelymitra (Orchidaceae)
Terrestrial orchids. Divide immediately following flowering. H9

Thelypteris (Thelypteridaceae)
Ferns of varying sizes. Divide as plants start into growth. H8

Thermopsis (Leguminosae)
Perennials of varying sizes, some of which can be difficult. Sow seed in spring after soaking in cold water for 24 hours. H8

Theropogon (Convallariaceae)
Perennials. Sow seed in spring, but if there is no germination exposure to winter cold can help. Divide after flowering. H8

Therorhodion camtschaticum now **Rhododendron camtschaticum**

Thlapsi (Cruciferae)
Annuals and perennials of varying qualities, some of which are weeds. Sow seed in spring. Divide as plants finish flowering. H7–8

Thuja (Cupressaceae)
Evergreen coniferous trees of which there are small cultivars. Take stem cuttings in winter and insert over bottom heat after wounding. H7–8

Thujopsis dolabrata (Pinaceae)
Coniferous tree or large shrub of which there are small cultivars suited to a large rock garden. Take stem cuttings in winter and insert over bottom heat after wounding. H8

Thymelaea (Thymelaeaceae)
Perennials and shrubs of varying sizes. Sow seed in spring. Take stem cuttings in autumn/fall. H8–9

Thymus (Labiatae)
Aromatic evergreen sub-shrubs of varying habits. Sow seed in spring. Take stem cuttings of non-flowering growth in summer. H7–9

Thysanotus (Anthericaceae)
Rhizomatous perennials, often sprawlers. Sow seed in spring. Divide as plants start into growth. H10

Tiarella (Saxifragaceae)
Perennials. Sow seed in spring. Divide as plants start into growth. H7

Tigridia (Iridaceae)
Bulbs that, with the exception of *T. pavonia*, are rather difficult. Sow seed in spring. Separate bulbs when dormant. H9

Tofieldia (Melanthiaceae)
Perennials of varying qualities. Best germination is from autumn/fall sown seed that is exposed to winter cold. Divide as plants start into growth. H6–7

Tolmiea menziesii (Saxifragaceae)
A perennial more curious than beautiful. Sow seed in spring. Divide as plants start into growth. Detach fully mature new leaves and treat as leaf cuttings. H8

Townsendia (Compositae)
Perennials, often short lived. Sow fertile seed in spring. H9

Trachelium (Campanulaceae)
Perennials that may become woody with age and of varying habits. Sow seed in spring. Take stem cuttings of new mature growth in late summer. H8–9

Tradescantia (Commeliniaceae)
Perennials of varying sizes and qualities. Sow seed in spring. Divide clump-formers as they start into growth. Take stem cuttings of non-flowering growth in autumn/fall. H7–9

Tremacron (Gesneriaceae)
Rhizomatous perennials. Sow seed in spring on chopped sphagnum moss. Take off fully mature new leaves and make into cuttings. H9

Trichinium see *Ptilotus*

Trichomanes (Hymenophyllaceae)
Creeping often epiphytic ferns. Divide when not in active growth. H8–10

Tricyrtis (Convallariaceae)
Perennials of varying sizes and habits, only a few of which are suited to a rock garden. Sow seed in spring. Divide as plants start into growth. H8–9

177

Trientalis (Primulaceae)
Perennials. Seed often has short viability. Sow as soon as collected in late summer or autumn/fall and expose to winter cold for best germination. Divide as plants start into growth. H7

Trifolium (Leguminosae)
A large genus of perennials of varying habits and qualities. Sow seed in spring; germination is improved if seed is soaked for 24 hours in cold water. Unless there is a single tap root, division can take place as plants start into growth. Take stem cuttings of non-flowering growth in autumn/fall. H8

Trillium (Trilliaceae)
Rhizomatous perennials. Sow seed in autumn/fall and expose to winter cold; germination can be delayed. Divide following flowering. H6–7

Trimezia (Iridaceae)
Corm. Sow seed in spring. Separate corms when not in active growth. H9

Tripetaleia (Ericaceae)
Small deciduous shrub. Sow seed in spring on chopped sphagnum moss. Take stem cuttings of new growth in early summer. H8

Triptilion (Compositae)
Annuals and perennials of varying habits. Sow fertile seed in spring. H8–9

Tristagma (Alliaceae)
Bulbs. Sow seed in spring. Separate bulbs when dormant. H8

Triteleia (Alliaceae)
Corms. Sow seed in spring. Separate corms when dormant. H8–9

Tritonia (Iridaceae)
Corms of varying sizes. Sow seed in spring. Separate corms when dormant. H8–9

Trochocarpa (Epacridaceae)
Low-growing small shrubs that are not easy. Sow seed in spring on chopped sphagnum moss; germination often difficult. Take stem cuttings in autumn/fall of non-flowering/fruiting growth; success variable.

Trollius (Ranunculaceae)
Perennials of varying sizes. Sow seed in summer as soon as it is ripe and expose to winter cold; germination can be erratic and delayed. Divide following flowering. H6

Tropaeolum (Tropaeoleaceae)
This genus, which includes annuals and perennials, is variable in habit and there are stoloniferous and tuberous species; only a few are suited to a rock garden. Seed has short viability and seems to do better with moist rather than dry storage. Sow seed as soon as possible after collecting. Tuberous species can be separated or divided when dormant. Stoloniferous kinds should be cut into pieces just before new growth begins. H8–10

Tsuga (Pinaceae)
Evergreen coniferous trees, although some species have produced small cultivars. Take stem cuttings in winter and insert over bottom heat after wounding; success is variable. H7

Tsusiophyllum tanakae (Ericaceae)
Small evergreen shrub. Sow seed in spring on chopped sphagnum moss. Take stem cuttings of non-flowering growth in autumn/fall. H8

Tuberaria (Cistaceae)
Annuals and perennials, often short lived. Sow seed in spring. Take cuttings of non-flowering growth in autumn/fall. H8

Tulbaghia (Alliaceae)
Perennials. Sow seed in spring. Divide as plants start into growth. H9

Tulipa (Liliaceae)
Summer-dormant bulbs of varying sizes, only some of which are suited to a rock garden. In general they do not naturalise and should be lifted annually. Sow seed in spring. Separate bulbs when dormant. H7–8

Tunica see *Petrorhagia*

Tweedia caerulea (Asclepiadaceae)
Sprawling evergreen sub-shrub. Sow seed in spring. H9–10

Ulex (Leguminosae)
Spiny leafless shrubs of varying sizes. Sow seed in spring after soaking in cold water for 24 hours. Take stem cuttings of new mature growth in autumn/fall. H7

Ulmus (Ulmaceae)
Large deciduous trees, but there are some very tiny cultivars suited to even the smallest rock garden. Take stem cuttings of new growth in late summer. H7

Umbilicus (Crassulaceae)
Succulent perennials with rhizomatous rootstock. Sow seed in spring. Divide as plants start into growth. H8

Uncinia (Cyperaceae)
Perennials with handsome foliage. Sow seed in spring. Divide as plants start into growth. H8

Ungernia (Amaryllidaceae)
Bulb. Sow seed in spring. Separate bulbs when dormant. Bulb cuttage; twin scaling. H9

Urceolina (Amaryllidaceae)
Bulb. Sow seed in spring. Separate bulbs when dormant. Twin scaling. H9

Urginea (Hyacinthaceae)
Summer-dormant bulbs of varying sizes, some too large for a rock garden. Sow seed in spring. Separate bulbs when dormant. Bulb cuttage; twin scaling. H9

Ursinia (Compositae)
Annuals, perennials and sub-shrubs. Sow fertile seed in spring. Take stem cuttings of non-flowering growth in autumn/fall. H9–10

Uvularia (Convallariaceae)
Rhizomatous perennials. Sow seed in spring. Divide following flowering. H7

Vaccinium (Ericaceae)
Deciduous and evergreen shrubs of varying sizes, habits and qualities. Sow seed in spring on chopped sphagnum moss. Take stem cuttings of non-flowering growth in autumn/fall. H6–9

Valeriana (Valerianaceae)
Perennials of varying sizes and qualities. Sow seed in spring. Divide as plants start into growth. H8

Vallota see *Cyrtanthus*

Vancouveria (Berberidaceae)
Perennial. Best germination from seed sown in autumn/fall after extracting from fruits and exposing to winter cold. Divide as new growth starts. H7–8

Vella (Cruciferae)
Evergreen or deciduous sub-shrubs. Sow seed in spring. Take stem cuttings in late summer. H8

Vellozia (Velloziaceae)
Perennials, the loose fans of which can become woody at the base. Sow seed in spring. Divide when not in active growth. H9–10

Velthemia (Hyacinthaceae)
Bulbs rather large for a rock garden. Sow seed in spring. Separate bulbs when dormant. Bulb cuttage; twin scaling. H8–9

Veratrum (Melanthiaceae)
Although many are botanical alpines, most are too large for a small rock garden. Sow seed in autumn/fall and expose to winter cold for best germination. Divide as plants start into growth. 7–8

Verbascum (Scrophulariaceae)
A large genus of varying sizes, habits and qualities, including annuals, biennials, perennials and sub-shrubs. Sow seed in spring. Divide clump-formers as they start into growth. Take stem cuttings of non-flowering growth in autumn/fall. Prepare root cuttings in late autumn/fall. H8–9

Verbena (Verbenaceae)
A large genus of varying habits and qualities, including annuals and perennials that may become woody at the base. Sow seed in spring. Take stem cuttings of non-flowering growth, if possible, in autumn/fall. H8–9

Veronica (Scrophulariaceae)
Perennials of varying sizes, habits and qualities. Sow seed in spring. Divide clump-formers as they start into growth. Take stem cuttings of non-flowering growth in autumn/fall. H8

Vicia (Leguminosae)
A large genus, including annuals and perennials of varying habits and qualities. Sow seed in spring after soaking for 24 hours in cold water. Division of some kinds is possible as plants start into growth. H7–8

Vinca (Apocynaceae)
Perennials and prostrate evergreen sub-shrubs of varying qualities. Sow seed in spring. Divide as plants start into growth. Take stem cuttings of non-flowering growth in summer. H8

Viola (Violaceae)
A large genus of annuals, perennials and sub-shrubs of varying habits and qualities. Sow seed in spring. Seed of the rossulate and ericoid species from South America contain chemical inhibitors. Soak for at least 24 hours in plenty of cold water; change the water several times during this period. Divide the spring-flowerers following blooming; the summer flowerers in spring as plants start into growth. Take stem cuttings in late summer or autumn/fall of non-flowering growth. Two or three weeks before taking cuttings cut back a few stems to provide suitable growth. Old flowering stems, which are hollow, are difficult to root. H7–9

Viscaria see *Lychnis*

Vittadenia (Compositae)
Perennials. Sow fertile seed in spring. Take stem cuttings of non-flowering growth in summer. H8–9

Vitalinia primuliflora (Now usually classified with *Androsace* [Primulaceae])
Perennial carpeter. Sow seed in spring. Divide as plants start into growth. Take stem cuttings in late summer. H9

Wahlenbergia (Campanulaceae)
A large genus, including annuals and perennials of varying habits and qualities; some are weedy. Sow seed in spring. Divide as plants start into growth. Take stem cuttings of non-flowering growth in autumn/fall. H8

Waldheimia (Compositae)
Perennials. Sow fertile seed, which can have low viability, in spring. H8

Waldsteinia (Rosaceae)
Usually creeping perennials. Sow seed in autumn/fall and expose to winter cold. Divide as plants start into growth. H7

Walleria (Tecophilaeaceae)
Tuberous perennials. Sow seed in spring, separate or divide when dormant. H9–10

Watsonia (Iridaceae)
Corms of varying sizes, most of which are too large for a rock garden. Sow seed in spring. Separate corms when dormant. H8–9

Weldenia candida (Commeliniaceae)
Perennial. Sow seed in spring. Divide as plants start into growth. H8–9

Werneria (Compositae)
Perennials. Sow fertile seed in spring. H8

Woodsia (Polypodiaceae)
Often creeping ferns. Divide when not in active growth. H8

Woodwardia (Blechnaceae)
Ferns with separate fertile fronds. Divide as plants start into growth. H8

Wulfenia (Scrophulariaceae)
Rhizomatous perennials. Sow seed in spring. Divide as plants start into growth. H8

Wurmbea (Colchicaceae)
Corms. Sow seed in spring. Separate corms when not in active growth. H9

Wyethia (Compositae)
Perennials. Sow fertile seed in spring. Divide as plants start into growth. Take stem cuttings in summer. H8

Xeronema callistemon (Phormiaceae)
Rhizomatous perennial that can become woody at the base. Sow seed in spring. Take off mature non-flowering fans, and if without roots treat as cuttings. H10

Xerophyllum (Melanthiaceae)
Rhizomatous perennial, rather large for a small rock garden; difficult. Sow seed in autumn/fall and expose to winter cold for best germination. H6

Xyris (Xyridaceae)
Perennials. Seed, which has a low fertility, should be sown as soon as available; germination can be delayed. Division can take place of established clumps as plants start into growth. H8–9

Yucca (Agavaceae)
Rosettes of leathery leaves on woody stems; most species are too large for a rock garden. Sow seed in spring. Take rosettes off the woody stems and treat as cuttings. H8–9

Zahlbruckneria paradoxa see *Saxifraga paradoxa*

Zaluzianskya (Scrophulariaceae)
Annuals and perennials, some species are night flowering. Sow seed in spring. H8–9

Zantedeschia (Araceae)
Tuberous perennials. Although the best known, *Z. aethiopica*, is too large for a rock garden, some of the other species would have a place on a larger rock garden. Sow seed in spring. Separate tubers when dormant and/or cut tubers into pieces. H8–9

Zapania see *Lippia*

Zauschneria (Onagraceae) (Now classified with *Epilobium*)
Perennials. Sow seed in spring. Take stem cuttings in late summer of non-flowering growth. H8–9

Zephyra elegans (Tecophileaeceae)
Corm. Sow seed in spring. Separate corms when dormant. H9

183

Zephyranthes (Amaryllidaceae)

Bulbs that flower best when crowded. Sow seeds in spring. Separate bulbs when dormant. Twin scaling. H8–9

Zigadenus (Mellanthiaceae)

Bulbs, in which all parts are poisonous. Sow seed in spring. Separate bulbs when dormant. H9

Appendix I   Societies

There are a number of societies dealing specifically with the cultivation of alpine plants, and several others devoted to a genus, many of whose representatives fall under this general heading. All of them run an annual seed exchange and produce a journal or yearbook. The majority also conduct a series of shows (The Alpine Garden Society, for example, currently holds 19 across England between March and October) or stage periodic exhibits at more generalised horticultural events such as those arranged by the Royal Horticultural Society.

The list that follows is not intended to be exhaustive, but suggests some of the more appropriate choices, whilst acknowledging the importance of specialist organisation elsewhere, notably the Prague Rock Garden Club and the Japanese Alpine Garden Society.

Alpine Garden Society (AGS)
Secretary: E. M. Upward,
Lye End Link, St John's, Woking,
Surrey GU21 1SW, England.

Alpine Club of British Columbia
Membership Chairman: Denys Lloyd,
3281 W. 35th Avenue, Vancouver VN
ZM9, British Columbia.

American Rock Garden Society
(ARGS)
Contact: Buffy Parker,
15 Fairmead Road, Darien,
Connecticut 06820 USA.

Botanical Society of South Africa
Contact: The Secretary,
Botanical Society of South Africa,
Claremont 7735, Cape, RSA.

Cyclamen Society
Contact: P. Moore
Tile Barn House, Standen Street,
Iden Green, Benenden, Kent
TN17 4LB, England

New Zealand Alpine Garden Society
Membership Secretary: Mrs A.
Lemmon,
17 Courage Road, Amberley,
New Zealand.

Saxifraga Group
Secretary: B. Arundel,
3 Pinewood Gardens, Hemel
Hempstead, Herts HP1 1TN,
England.

Scottish Rock Garden Club
(SRGC)
Subscription Secretary: Miss K. M.
Gibb,
21 Merchiston Park, Edinburgh
EH10 4PW, Scotland.

Appendix II Sources of Plants and Seed

Relatively few nurseries specialise in plants for the alpine gardener. But, despite fears to the contrary prompted by the difficulties relating to their propagation and the additional time often taken to produce a saleable plant, an ever-widening range of suitable species is being offered for sale. Tracking them down to their disparate sources can be a lengthy business, notwithstanding the emergence of directories such as *The Plant Finder*, since the rarer species are not always catalogued, and it is a question of making speculative enquiries.

The following list gives an indication of some established sources, but new nurseries are continually springing up. Not all are able to export, nor even to send their plants through the post, which is where the seed merchants score. Such sources make a vast range of material available to enthusiasts, who may not necessarily live in countries where the cultivation of alpine plants has developed sufficiently to see the opening of specialist nurseries.

In addition, there are 'one-off' seed collections made by individuals or small parties who can be contacted by scanning the advertisement section of specialist society journals.

As contacts build up and collections are established, exchange of material between one gardener and another, quite frequently on an international basis, is likely to be of greater significance. Subject to the constraints governing the removal of plants from the wild, modest introductions from this source can be established and, it is to be hoped, distributed to other interested parties.

Alpine Plant Nurseries (UK)

Ardfearn Nursery, Bunchren, Inverness IV3 6RH, Scotland.

R. F. Beeston, 294 Ombersley Road, Worcester WR3 7HD.

Blackthorn Nursery, Kilmeston, Alresford, Hants SO24 0NL. (*Daphne*, persona callers only.)

Broadleigh Gardens, Barr House, Bishop's Hull, Taunton, Somerset TA4 1AE (Hardy bulbs.)

Butterfields Nursery, Harvest Hill, Bourne End, Bucks SL8 5JJ. (*Pleione*.)

Cambridge Bulbs (C. F. and N. J. Stevens), 40 Whittlesford Road, Newton, Cambridge CB2 5PA. (*Crocus, Fritillaria, Iris*.)

K. W. Davis, Brook House, Lingen, Nr Bucknell, Craven Arms, Shropshire SY7 0DY.

186

Jack Drake, Inshriach Alpine Plant Nursery, Aviemore, Invernessshire PH22 1QS, Scotland.

Edrom Nurseries (Propr. J. Jermyn), Coldingham, Eyemouth, Berwickshire TD14 5TZ, Scotland.

Highgates Alpines (R. E. and D. I. Straughan), 166A Crich Lane, Belper, Derbyshire DE5 1EP. (Personal callers only.)

Holden Clough Nursery (P. J. Foley), Holden, Bolton-by-Bowland, Clitheroe, Lancs BB7 4PF.

W. E. Th. Ingwersen Ltd, Birch Farm Nursery, Gravetye, E. Grinstead, W. Sussex RH19 4LE.

L. Kreeger, 91 Newton Wood Road, Ashtead, Surrey KT21 1NN. (Also issues a seed list.)

Potterton & Martin, The Cottage Nursery, Moortown Road, Nettleton, Nr Caistor, N. Lincolnshire LN7 6HX.

M. Salmon, Monocot Seeds, Jacklands Bridge, Twickenham, Avon BS21 6SG. (Bulbous plants, seed list.)

D. Sampson, Oakdene Nursery, Scotsford Road, Broadoak, Heathfield, E. Sussex TN21 8TU.

Tile Barn Nursery, Standen Street, Eden Green, Benenden, Kent TN17 4LB. (*Cyclamen.*)

Waterperry Horticultural Centre, Alpine Dept, Nr Wheatley, Oxon OX9 1JL. (*Saxifraga.*)

Commercial Seed Lists (UK)

Jim and Jenny Archibald, 'Bryn Collen', Ffostrasol, Llandysul, Dyfed, SA44 5SN, Wales. (Field collected seed - Europe, Turkey, Northwest USA – also from cultivated stock.)

C. Chadwell, 81 Parlaunt Road, Slough, Berks SL3 8BE. (Himalayan genera.)

Chiltern Seeds, Bortree Style, Ulverston, Cumbria LA12 7PB.

L. Kreeger (see nursery list).

Monocot Seeds (see nursery list).

Northside Seeds, Ludlow House, 12 Kingsley Avenue, Kettering, Northants NN16 9EU.

Rocky Mountain Rare Plants, PO Box 20483, Denver, Colorado 80220-0483, USA.

Southern Seeds, The Vicarage, Sheffield, Canterbury, New Zealand.

Southwestern Seeds, PO Box 50503, Tucson, Arizona 85703, USA.

Woodbank Nursery (see nursery list).

D. & A. Wraight, 25 rue Paul Eyschen, L-7317 Steinsel, G. D. Luxembourg. (Seed collected in the Andes.)

Alpine Plant Suppliers (USA) _____

Campana Nursery, Huon Highway, Longley, Tasmania 7103.

Colorado Alpines Inc., PO Box 2708, Avon, CO 81620.

Hokanui Alpines, Croydon Side Road, Gore, Southland, New Zealand.

Jack Scott, 220 Pine Hill Road, Dunedin, Otago, New Zealand.

Lamb's Nurseries, E.101 Sharp Avenue, Spokane, Washington 99202.

Kereru Nursery, Okuti Valley, Little River, Canterbury, New Zealand.

Maple Glen, Glenham, Wyndham, Southland, New Zealand.

Mt Tahoma Nursery, 28111-112th Avenue East, Graham, Washington 98338.

Oliver Nurseries Inc., 1159 Bronson Road, Fairfield, CT 06430.

Rice Creek Gardens Inc., 1315 66th Avenue Northeast, Minneapolis, Minnesota 55432.

Rocknoll Nursery, 9210 US 50, Hillsboro, Ohio 45133-8546.

Rocky Mountain Rare Plants, PO Box 20483, Denver, CO 80220-0483.

Russell Graham, 4030 Eagle Crest Road Northwest, Salem, Oregon 97304.

Siskiyou Rare Plant Nursery, 2825 Cummings Road, Medford, Oregon 97501.

Appendix III Conversion Tables

Bold figures in the central columns can be read as either metric or imperial: e.g., 1 kg = 2.20 lb or 1 lb = 0.45 kg.

mm		in	cm		in	m		yds
25.4	1	0.039	2.54	1	0.39	0.91	1	1.09
50.8	2	0.079	5.08	2	0.79	1.83	2	2.19
76.2	3	0.118	7.62	3	1.18	2.74	3	3.28
101.6	4	0.157	10.16	4	1.57	3.66	4	4.37
127.0	5	0.197	12.70	5	1.97	4.57	5	5.47
152.4	6	0.236	15.24	6	2.36	5.49	6	6.56
177.8	7	0.276	17.78	7	2.76	6.40	7	7.66
203.2	8	0.315	20.32	8	3.15	7.32	8	8.75
228.6	9	0.354	22.86	9	3.54	8.23	9	9.84

g		oz	kg		lb	km		miles
28.35	1	0.04	0.45	1	2.20	1.61	1	0.62
56.70	2	0.07	0.91	2	4.41	3.22	2	1.24
85.05	3	0.11	1.36	3	6.61	4.83	3	1.86
113.40	4	0.14	1.81	4	8.82	6.44	4	2.48
141.75	5	0.18	2.27	5	11.02	8.05	5	3.11
170.10	6	0.21	2.72	6	13.23	9.65	6	3.73
198.45	7	0.25	3.18	7	15.43	11.26	7	4.35
226.80	8	0.28	3.63	8	17.64	12.87	8	4.97
255.15	9	0.32	4.08	9	19.84	14.48	9	5.59

ha		acres	Metric to imperial conversion formulae	
0.40	1	2.47		multiply by
0.81	2	4.94	cm to inches	0.3937
1.21	3	7.41	m to feet	3.281
1.62	4	9.88	m to yards	1.094
2.02	5	12.36	km to miles	0.6214
2.43	6	14.83	km^2 to square miles	0.3861
2.83	7	17.30	ha to acres	2.471
3.24	8	19.77	g to ounces	0.03527
3.64	9	22.24	kg to pounds	2.205

Bibliography

Bean, W. J. *Trees and Shrubs Hardy in the British Isles*, 5 vols (J. Murray, 1970–88)

Bird, R. W. *Guide to Rock Gardening* (Christopher Helm, 1990)

Chittenden, F. J. *The RHS Dictionary of Gardening*, 4 vols, plus 2 supplements (Clarendon Press, 1950–69)

Clay, S. *The Present Day Rock Garden* (T. C. & E. C. Jack, 1937)

Evans, A. (ed.) *Alpines '81* (1981 International Rock Garden Conference Report) (Alpine Garden Society and Scottish Rock Garden Club, 1981)

Farrer, R. *The English Rock Garden*, 2 vols (Thomas Nelson, 1919)

Flint, G. J. & Hanks, G. R. *Twin Scaling and Chipping Virus Free Bulbs in Bulk* (The Grower, 4/2/82)

Garner, R. *The Grafter's Handbook*, 2nd edition (Faber, 1967)

Grey-Wilson, C. *A Manual of Alpine and Rock Garden Plants* (Christopher Helm, 1989)

Hartmann, H. T. & Kester, D. E. *Plant Propagation, Principles and Practices*, 2nd edition (Prentice-Hall, 1968)

Hills, L. D. *The Propagation of Alpines* (Faber, 1950)

Ingwersen, W. *Manual of Alpine Plants* (Collingridge, 1978)

Mabberley, D. J. *The Plant Book* (Cambridge University Press, 1989)

Mathew, B. *Dwarf Bulbs* (Batsford, 1973)

Mathew, B. *The Larger Bulbs* (Batsford, 1978)

Mathew, B. *The Smaller Bulbs* (Batsford, 1987)

Macdonald, B. *Woody Plant Propagation for Nursery Growers* (Batsford, 1986)

Rix, M. *Growing Bulbs* (Croom Helm, 1983)

Rolfe, R. *The Alpine House* (Christopher Helm, 1990)

Sheat, W. G. *Propagation of Trees, Shrubs and Conifers* (Macmillan, 1948)

Sutton, S. (ed.) *Alpines of the Americas* (1975) International Rock Garden Conference Report (American Rock Garden Society and Alpine Garden Bulb of British Columbia, 1976)

Willis, J. C. *Dictionary of Flowering Plants and Ferns* (Cambridge University Press, 1973 edition)

Flora Europea, 5 vols (Cambridge University Press, 1964–80)

Woody Plant Seed Manual (Forestry Service of United States Department of Agriculture, 1948)

Journals

Alpine Garden Club of British Columbia

Alpine Garden Society (and other of its publications)

American Rock Garden Soceity

New Zealand Alpine Garden Society

The Scottish Rock Garden Club

Index